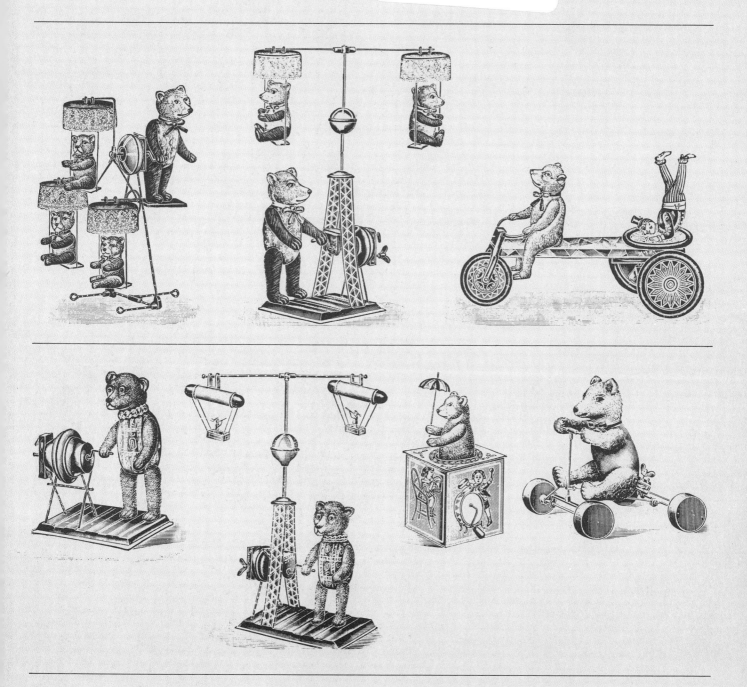

Collecting
TEDDY BEARS

Collecting
TEDDY BEARS

PAM HEBBS

COLLINS

ACKNOWLEDGEMENTS
Many people have contributed to the preparation and writing of this book, but I should like to acknowledge especially the help and encouragement I received from Carol Hebbs, whose enthusiasm for the project and support during its writing were unfailing. The contribution of Linda Ayres is also gratefully acknowledged. I should also like to take this opportunity to thank Roy Gasson and Nick Nicholson for their editorial and photographic skills.

I should also like to acknowledge John Murray (Publishers) Ltd, who granted permission to reproduce the quotation from John Betjeman's *Summoned by Bells*, which appears on page 7; and Curtis Brown Ltd, London, who granted permission to reproduce pages from *Winnie the Pooh* and *Winnie Ille Pu*, which may be seen on page 133 (text by A. A. Milne and drawings by E. H. Shephard are copyright under the Berne Convention).

Text © Pam Hebbs 1988

First published in 1988 by
William Collins Sons & Co. Ltd
London · Glasgow · Sydney
Auckland · Toronto · Johannesburg

British Library Cataloguing in Publication Data

Hebbs, Pam
    Collecting teddy bears. – (Collecting series).
    1. Teddy bears – Collectors and collecting
    I. Title   II. Series
    745.592'4   GV1220.7
    ISBN 0-00-412274-7

Produced by
Justin Knowles Publishing Group,
9 Colleton Crescent, Exeter, Devon
EX2 4BY

Design: Peter Wrigley
Photography: Nick Nicholson

Typeset by Typesetters (Birmingham) Ltd
Printed and bound in Britain by
Purnell Book Production Ltd

FRONTISPIECE
On the left of this group of new bears is a 1970 Zotty. Next to it is a white Steiff made in 1984, while the golden bear on the right was made by Steiff for the Margaret Woodbury Strong Museum, Washington, in 1985. The small golden Steiff in front of the group was also made in 1984. (**£40–80; $60–130**) *Private collection*

CONTENTS

Two British postcards sent as Christmas greetings: the left-hand card was posted in 1912, the one on the right in 1920 — an indication of the early popularity achieved by teddy bears.

Safe were those evenings of the pre-war world
When firelight shone on green linoleum;
I heard the church bells hollowing out the sky,
Deep beyond deep, like never-ending stars,
And turned to Archibald, my safe old bear,
Whose woollen eyes looked sad or glad at me,
Whose ample forehead I could wet with tears,
Whose half-moon ears received my confidence,
Who made me laugh, who never let me down.
I used to wait for hours to see him move,
Convinced that he could breathe. One dreadful day
They hid him from me as a punishment:
Sometimes the desolation of that loss
Comes back to me and I must go upstairs
To see him in the sawdust, so to speak,
Safe and returned to his idolater.

John Betjeman
Summoned by Bells (1960)

FOREWORD

I suppose I might rightly claim to have been one of the earliest teddy-bear collectors and as such to be well qualified to introduce the subject. In Britain in the early 1920s, soon after World War I had ended, toys were scarce but there were tiny teddy bears that were beautiful, many coloured, and cheap. They came in various shades of brown and gold and in white and pink and cost only one shilling (5p) each. It was not difficult at that time to furnish a whole dolls' house with a family of bears, even on limited pocket money. When my older brothers fitted out and decorated the interior of a large Chinese lacquer cupboard my bears moved in. It became a house on two shelves, with linoleum on the floors, pretty wallpaper, and mock curtained windows. It was provided with chunky furniture and miniature pots and pans so that the bears could sit comfortably at their lunch.

But times have changed and bears have changed. Recently, at a doll and toy fair, I saw a little bear like mine, a shabby antique priced at £30!

Psychologically, why people should become collectors of teddy bears has still to be studied and explained. It is simple to understand the appeal of the single bear that is the first toy of childhood, a soft friend clasped by a toddler. When, some years ago, I helped stage a museum exhibition of teddies, the elderly owners who wandered in, curious, usually volunteered that they wanted to put their old friend "on show". It was an exercise in nostalgia. The toy recalled childhood in its happiest (or loneliest) moments. The bear was their perfect surrogate brother, sister, pet, snuggled up to and confided in. The owners were reluctant to part with their bears (or their memories). They had been together for perhaps seventy years and would never part. Never? Now that the auction houses can obtain £3,000 for a really fine example in good condition, obviously a temptation arises. I have seen folk in tears as they left their bear at the counter to be sold. "He will be going to a good home," I promise them, "where he will be loved and admired".

But what motivates the collectors? Perhaps they never shared their home with a bear friend, but now seek 30 such old friends, or 300, or even 3,000. How many teddy bears make sense? Are they all loved, all valuable, (all hygienic)?

In this book, Pam Hebbs, herself a committed collector, gives some of the answers. First there is the competitive element, which has been promoted by the dealers in toys and dolls and advertised by various magazines. Then there has been vast publicity by some of the charitable organizations that have become involved. The hunt is on to find the oldest, the rarest, the largest. This has certainly produced a lot of research in the rather uncertain origins of the toy bear.

Of the assorted bears seen opposite, the two larger teddies were made by Schuco. The dressed bear on the left has a metal body covered by cloth, and the hat and trousers are an integral part of the body. The bear still has its original trade label and was made in 1937. The right-hand Schuco bear, which dates from about 1948, has a swivel head, moved by pulling its tail. *Private collection*

A few steps further on and one may add all the wealth of teddy-bear related material. In its hey-day, before 1914, printed china, postcards, mechanical tin toys, songs, buttons, and baubles were all decorated with the beloved image. Presently the artists and the authors took over and gave the teddy bear a whole library of literature and gallery of pictures. The committed collector may like to include Rupert as the most famous, or go on to add Paddington Bear and television stars such as Sooty. The parade goes on. How, for instance, must we class Care Bears, formidable rivals to older teddies with modern juveniles who can follow on their television screens the sugary moral antics of this gang? Antiques of the future perhaps, when their ranks have thinned.

It is interesting to remember that the very first stuffed bears were made by hand, whether by the talented Margarete Steiff in Germany or the enterprising, candy-selling Michtoms in America. There are some splendid hand-made bears, artist-crafted, still and they are worth collecting and often unique.

Pam Hebbs has given useful guidelines for finding your bears and distinguishing their pedigree, even down to detecting fakes. She has rightly suggested, as a likely source for bears, some well-intentioned Granny (or Grandpa), but such endearing relics may be as difficult to find as the bears themselves and elderly relatives nowadays are probably well aware of sensational saleroom prices and may even have an over-optimistic idea of the value of their treasures.

The chapter on the care and repair of ancient bears is not for the squeamish, and the mere thought of putting his own beloved Theodore in a refrigerator would have quite devastated that lovable bearman, the late Peter Bull. Some ingenious chemist will, I am sure, soon promote a special brand of cleaner/disinfectant for old bears – MEDI-TED?

Bears nowadays not only "look sad or glad" at you, they probably sing a few songs or answer back to questions. Myself, I like a mixture of modern ingenuity with the old, but whether you furnish just a corner of the room, a whole room, or a whole house with a teddy-bear collection, enjoy it and especially remember to back your own fancy. As Pam Hebbs points out, buying an old teddy is rather like buying a puppy. If one appeals to you no amount of advice will deter you from owning it.

Good luck!

MARY HILLIER

INTRODUCTION

Teddy bears have been loved by children for almost a hundred years. For the greater part of that time they stayed in the nursery where they were thought to belong. Giving up the toys of infancy was, for boys, one of the stages on the road to manhood.

> When nine, I hid you in the loft
> And dared not let you share my bed;
> My father would have thought me soft,
> So at least my mother said.
>   (John Betjeman. *Uncollected Poems*)

But there have always been those who have carried their childhood teddy bears with them into adult life. Teddy bears accompanied Royal Air Force pilots into aerial dogfights in the Battle of Britain and GIs to

Three more British postcards, these dating from the early 1920s. The one on the left was sent as a Valentine's Day greeting.

The family group (above) was photographed at Belshill, England, in July 1909; the photograph of the two huge bears enjoying a seaside holiday is, unfortunately, undated.

Vietnam. But there was always a faint feeling of shame, a tendency to secrecy, surrounding the clinging in this way to a childhood toy.

Then, quite suddenly it seems, adult teddy-bear aficionados came out of the closet. One of the leaders of this movement was a British actor, Peter Bull. At a dinner party in New York in the mid-1960s one of the guests told him that, as a girl of eight, she was travelling by train across Europe with her parents, when a customs officer, searching for contraband, had grabbed her teddy bear, slit it open and decapitated it. She said that she had never got the incident out of her mind. "At the time," Peter Bull wrote, "my main feeling was one of astonishment that I was not the only person in the world with a Teddy Bear secret! Mine being that my mother had disposed of my beloved friend one term-time to a local Jumble Sale." He began to invite confidences about teddy bears and quickly discovered "the intensity of the emotion felt by some adults when discussing their stuffed animals". He wrote a book, *Bear with me (The Teddy Bear Book* in the United States), published in 1969, which stimulated, or perhaps merely uncovered, a wide interest in the teddy bear and began a cult.

Other books followed in Peter Bull's tracks. Serious research into the history and background of the teddy bear was generated. The teddy bear became accepted as a worthwhile collectible – and began to be seen as potentially a very valuable one. As a consequence – particularly as professional dealers moved into the collecting scene – the teddy became an object of study from a more sophisticated viewpoint, like any other antique.

So today's teddy-bear collector needs to be informed and knowledge-able. *Collecting Teddy Bears* is intended to be that collector's handbook, companion, and guide.

The Bully Bear "family" listening to
Peter Bull reading from his famous
Teddy Bear Book, a Limited
Signature Edition

1.
WHAT IS A TEDDY BEAR?

The teddy bear has been described as the world's most popular soft toy. More than 60 per cent of all British households have one, and, at a conservative estimate, there are more than 140 million of them in the United States. And yet it is a soft toy invented, as we shall see in Chapter 2, less than a century ago. The phenomenal popularity of the teddy bear over these years demonstrates that it is rather more than a child's plaything.

Nonetheless, it is basically simply a cuddly toy. So what accounts for its success?

One theory is that it came on to the market at a time when there was a great need for toys for boys, dolls being considered unsuitable and unmanly. It does seem true that boys have been as attached to the teddy bear as have girls – indeed it perhaps appeals more to boys simply because to them the alternative of a doll has not been available. One reason for the bear-boy relationship may be that the teddy bear – like most animal toys – seems to be neither male nor female. It is also much tougher than a doll, which seems to exist only to be cared for. A teddy bear can be treated with affectionate toughness, like a friend. And bears are seen as warmer and more responsive. Peter Bull, in *Bear with me*, thought that "a security blanket is far nearer to the bear in temperament, as it at least affords comfort to a comparable degree. A doll seems to be (in my eyes) pretty vain and totally egotistic. The Teddy has physical qualities which make an immediate unselfish appeal. One knows instinctively that they are there to help and woe betide the person, of whatever age, suddenly deprived of their services."

Very early on in the teddy bear's history, in 1907, a Boston journalist, Caroline Tickner, writing in the *New England Magazine*, with great prescience saw it all:

Nancy Carroll and friend. *Courtesy the Museum of Modern Art Stills Archive, New York*

The Teddy Bear has come to stay, so perfectly is his grizzly exterior adapted to fitting into the many chubby arms which are extended to him. He is not only bear-like enough to lift him above juvenile criticism but he is possessed of those semi-human attributes which fit him eminently for youthful companionship. He is every inch a bear and yet he certainly embodies exactly the doll qualities which are demanded by the child of to-day. He is well-made and set up. His head really turns round and his legs are nicely adjustable. He has moreover that precious gift of true adaptability; he can be made to crawl, climb, stand or sit and in each pose he is not only delightfully himself but he also suggests to the imaginative owner whatever special being his fancy would have his teddy personify.

In *Dear Octopus*, a play by British dramatist Dodie Smith that had a long run in London's West End in the 1930s, there is a scene in which a prodigal daughter, Cynthia, returns to her family home and, going into the nursery, finds a child called Scrap. There is also a teddy bear:

CYNTHIA   Is that a teddy bear? Why, it's Symp!
SCRAP   Symp?
CYNTHIA   We call him that because he was extra sympathetic. We used to hug him whenever we were miserable, when we were in disgrace or the rabbits died or when nobody understood us.
SCRAP   Did Mummy hug him?
CYNTHIA   We all did. It went on till we were quite big. Hello, Symp, my lad, how did you lose that arm?
SCRAP   Is he still sympathetic?
CYNTHIA   He looks it to me. His fur used to get sopping wet with tears. Oh, comfortable Symp! He must be over thirty years old.

That is teddy bear as comforter. Psychologists have seen it also as a father figure representing to the child goodness, benevolence, and kindness.

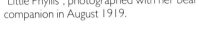

"Little Phyllis", photographed with her bear companion in August 1919.

A British bear collector and bear authority, Colonel Robert Henderson (see page 43), writing in the magazine *Bear Tracks* in 1977, said:

> From early times the bear has commanded a special place in folklore, myth, fairy-tale and legend. It has been regarded as a representative of both divine and natural forces; and today, in the form of the Teddy Bear, it is grasped in psychic compensation and clung to for security. The reason for this is that the bear functions as a powerful symbol that provides satisfaction for a widespread psychological need. Consequently, history, religion, philosophy and psychology are all involved in any proper explanation of the Teddy Bear.

In summation – and he shall have the last word – Colonel Henderson said that the teddy bear "plays a great part in the psychological development of many people of all ages all over the world. This because he is a truly international figure that is non-religious and yet is universally recognised as a symbol of love and affection. He represents friendship. . . . He functions as a leavening influence amid the trials and tribulations of life."

LEFT
A fairly typical 1930s photograph: the proud owner of a rather aloof-looking bear.

OVERLEAF
This Steiff bear, which dates from about 1910, is pictured here beside a photograph of the little girl who originally owned it. Finding such documentary evidence of a bear's provenance is always exciting and can add to its value. The bear is 18in (46cm) tall. (**£200–500; $330–825**) *Author's collection*

2.
A SHORT HISTORY OF TEDDY BEARS

The godfather of the teddy bear was Theodore Roosevelt, 26th president of the United States. He was handicapped in his childhood by asthma and, perhaps in compensation, as a young man he made a gospel of physical fitness. As part of the macho image he cultivated he became a dedicated big-game hunter. By the time he became president, upon the assassination in 1901 of president William McKinley, he had written several books on hunting game in America and Africa. So when, in November 1902, he was in the American South to arbitrate in a border dispute between the states of Louisiana and Mississippi, it was not unnatural that he should take time off to go bear hunting in Mississippi. The grizzlies he sought were, though, uncooperative and after several days Roosevelt had made no kill. His embarrassed hosts searched the woods for a bear for the president to shoot at, and eventually flushed out a bear cub which they drove towards his camp. Roosevelt was contemptuous; he refused to shoot so small and pitiful a sitting target. His humanity, however, did not extend to saving the bear's life; it was dispatched by a hunter's knife.

The press was in attendance and the incident was reported. Clifford K.

ONE OF US MUST DIE.

LEFT
This 1908 postcard – entitled "One of us must die" – was addressed to "Miss Seddon's teddy bear" at 28 Crediton Road, London N.W., and it carries the cryptic message "Smeller Sint: here's a p.c."

OPPOSITE
These are two early mechanical bears. The white one climbs up the ladder (which is not original to the bear); it is French and was made about 1910. The brown bear, also French, was made by Martin about 1890. Both bears are very rare. (**£200–400; $330–660**) *Author's collection*

Berryman, then a cartoonist for the *Washington Post*, went one step beyond straight reportage and related the affair to the president's political mission. He drew a cartoon, captioned "Drawing the Line in Mississippi", depicting Roosevelt rejecting, with upraised hand, the opportunity to shoot at close range a small, tethered, terrified bear.

The cartoon attracted widespread and favourable attention in Washington and New York. It caught the public eye. Berryman drew at least one other version of the original and adopted the bear as a motif in several later political cartoons in which he charted the remainder of Roosevelt's presidency. Roosevelt, too, for the rest of his career capitalized upon the event and took the bear as his motif and mascot. The bear became so closely identified with him that when, on a visit to England in June 1910, he went to Oxford, undergraduates put a welcoming teddy bear in his path. We have it on the authority of his daughter Alice, though, that Roosevelt was never very taken by teddy bears. He used them but did not much like them. She inherited this trait from him; when, in her eighties, she gave an interview to the British actor and teddy-bear propagandist Peter Bull, she insisted that he bring no teddy bears with him, because she hated them.

But if the teddy bear has an American president as its godfather, who was its father? This is more difficult, but there are two main contenders for paternity.

One of the people who saw the Berryman cartoon was a Russian immigrant, Morris Michtom, who, with his wife, ran a small confectionery, novelty, and stationery shop in Brooklyn, New York. It struck him as an idea to cash in on the affair by offering for sale a stuffed toy bear. Mrs Michtom made the first bear, which had movable arms and legs and was plush-covered. They put it in their shop window. It sold, quickly. Mrs Michtom made more to replace it. Sales escalated. Butler Brothers, one of the largest toy wholesalers in the United States, undertook its distribution and underwrote the Michtoms' credit with their suppliers. Within a year the bear had achieved impressive sales.

At roughly the same time, in Germany, a small family firm of toy makers added a stuffed bear to its range of soft toys. The Steiff Company's best seller up to then had been a stuffed-elephant pincushion. This was the original creation of the firm's founder and guiding light, Margarete Steiff. Born in 1847, Margarete was a childhood victim of polio, which left her legs paralysed and weakened her left arm. But she was eager to be independent and to earn her own living, and she learned to sew. She became a seamstress in the little town of Giengen-am-Brenz in Würtemburg where she lived. While still a teenager, she opened her own dress shop, selling clothes she had made using materials from her uncle's felt factory. Then she had the idea of the elephant pincushion. These sold well in the neighbourhood. Her brother Fritz took them to fairs and there, too, they sold well. Soon Margarete and her by now growing band of helpers were offering other stuffed animals as well – camels, monkeys, donkeys, horses, and pigs. By 1893 the firm had grown big enough to

This Steiff skittle bear (which is also illustrated on pages 42 and 67) is one of a set of nine different animals with the bear as king. This rather unusual bear dates from about 1898. It is 10in (26cm) high and is in mint condition. (**£200–400; $330–660**)
Private collection

A rare silver bear made by Steiff about 1905. It is 30in (76cm) high. When it was sold at auction in October 1985 it fetched £3,400 ($5,610). *Sotheby's*

exhibit its products for the first time at the prestigious Leipzig Toy Fair.

The stuffed bear that brings Steiff into the teddy-bear story was made at the insistence of one of Margarete's nephews, Richard. He had studied sculpture at Stuttgart. There he had spent happy hours studying the antics of bear cubs at the zoo and watching the performing bears at Hagenbeck's Circus. He had sketched bears in every conceivable pose. He entered his aunt's flourishing company in 1879. Years later he went back

A Steiff bear made about 1904. It is 27in (69cm) high and has yellow fur and a button in its ear. This bear is in particularly nice condition, and it was sold for £720 ($1,188) in October 1985. *Sotheby's*

to his Stuttgart sketches and designed a new toy bear. Margarete, apparently, was not greatly impressed. The firm had already produced bears standing on four legs and an upright dancing bear. They had not been greatly successful. Richard argued, however, that his bear was different. It had a movable head and movable limbs and it could be dressed, could be cuddled, could be loved. He made his point and the first prototype bears were manufactured.

The new Steiff bears were shown at the Leipzig Toy Fair of 1903. But before that a sample had been sent to the United States where Paul Steiff, another of Margarete's seemingly endless supply of nephews, was given the spare-time job of stimulating interest in this new bear and of finding a representative to sell it in America. But Paul met with nothing but ridicule. He was told that the bear was too thick, fat, and clumsy; someone even called it a stuffed misfit. Although the bear was altered and streamlined, in response to Paul's market-research findings, before it was shown at the Leipzig Fair, none of the buyers there showed any interest in it. Then, on the last day of the Fair, a buyer from one of the biggest New York toy importers, George Borgfeldt & Co., went up to the Steiff representatives and told them how disappointed he was to have found

RIGHT
This Steiff bear, 26in (66cm) high and dating from about 1908, is one of the author's personal favourites. An earlier owner must have moved its ears! (**£1,500–1,800; $2,475–2,970**) *Author's collection*

OPPOSITE
All the bears shown here date from before 1920; all, except the white bear, which is a Bing, are by Steiff. (**£300–1,000; $495–1,650**) *Author's collection*

nothing particularly new or exciting at the Fair; what he wanted, he said, was something new, something soft and cuddly. Richard Steiff produced his bear, and took an immediate order for 3,000. (Steiff legend has it that the Borgfeldt man was so overcome that he did not even stop to ask the price, but this takes us beyond the limits of credulity.) The initial American response to the bears was so good that the order was quickly doubled, and by the end of the year 1903, Steiff had sold 12,000 bears. The next few years were a bear boom time. In 1907 Steiff bear production reached 974,000. The company still looks back on that year as the *Bärenjahre*, the Year of the Bear.

Whether Steiff in Germany or Michtom in the United States should be hailed as the inventor of the teddy bear has exercised the minds of writers

OPPOSITE AND BELOW
Not only is this bear a bright cinnamon, a rare colour, but it also has a centre seam, which is said to have been used for the earliest Steiff bears. It was made about 1905 and stands 26in (66cm) high. (**£1,000–3,000; $1,650–4,950**) *Author's collection*

and enthusiasts for many years. But it seems unnecessary to champion the cause of either claimant at the expense of the other. It is almost always a historical error to assume that there must be only one, unique, inventor. There seems no reason to doubt that the Michtoms produced a toy bear at the right time and that the Steiff company did the same. No doubt other, now forgotten, toy companies in Europe and America were at the time producing toy bears in various shapes, sizes, and materials.

When did these bear novelties first acquire the name "teddy bears"? Morris Michtom is said to have labelled the first bear in his shop window "Teddy's Bear" and to have shown it, by way of explanation, alongside Berryman's cartoon. Then, the story goes, his conscience pricked him. A refugee from an authoritarian country, and perhaps oversensitive because of that, he was concerned at making unsanctioned use of the president's name. So he sent a sample bear to Roosevelt and asked permission to call it "Teddy Bear" in memory of the Mississippi hunting episode. The president replied, in his own handwriting, and with becoming modesty, that he did not think his name was worth much to the toy-bear business, but that Mr Michtom was welcome to use it. Neither the Michtom letter nor the president's reply, though, has ever been produced in evidence and this tale, pleasant though it is, is without much doubt apocryphal.

The original Steiff bear was not, of course, called "Teddy". It was a German bear and it had a German name, *Petz*. So how to account for a German bear acquiring an American name? Back we go to another Roosevelt story. In 1906 the president's daughter Alice (she who many years later proclaimed to Peter Bull her antipathy to teddy bears) was to be married. The caterer for the occasion was wracking his brains to think of a suitable motif to decorate the tables for the wedding breakfast. In a New York store window he spotted a Steiff bear. Realizing immediately that this was the answer to his problem, he dashed in and bought several of the little bears. Dressed as hunters or fishermen, carrying rifles or fishing rods, the bears decorated the wedding tables and drew much favourable comment from the guests. One of them asked the father of the bride what kind of bear they were. Roosevelt confessed himself at a loss, but another guest explained that they were a new species called "Teddy".

This unlikely story is, of course, pure myth.

None the less it seems certain that the bears were in America called "Teddy" bears after Roosevelt, but that the connection rests simply on the Mississippi episode and the Berryman cartoon and was probably encouraged by Roosevelt's campaign aides (he was elected for a second term in 1905), who saw it as a useful political symbol.

Britain seems to have accepted the name from America, although it does have its own teddy-bear myth. It is that the king, Edward VII, took a particular liking to an Australian koala bear in the London zoo and that, in his honour, the animal became known as "Teddy bear". It is perhaps over-pedantic to point out that the koala is not a bear but a marsupial, but fair to state that there is no evidence whatever to back up this story. It

Two of the first bears in the author's collection were this 1905 Steiff with a button in its ear and the Dean's bear. Most bears seem to be "boys", but this Dean's bear has such a sweet face that it was dressed as a bride. The Steiff is 17in (43cm) high, the Dean's bear 16in (41cm) high.
(£700–1,400 the pair; $1,155–2,310)
Author's collection

may well have been invented purely to provide background for a laboured punning joke about Edward's mistress, Lillie Langtry – that she preferred her Teddy bear.

The editors both of Webster's dictionaries in the United States and of the Oxford dictionaries in Britain agree in recording the first instance of the term "teddy bear" as occurring in 1907. This is doubtless correct in terms of literature, but in the toy trade at least the use of the term can be pushed back a few months into 1906. In an American toy-trade magazine, *Playthings*, an advertisement of May 1906 for a range of "jointed plush bears" appeared under the heading "We told you this was Bruin's Day". It nowhere uses the term "teddy bear". But in November of the same year, in the same magazine, the toy manufacturer E. I. Horsman describes his products as "Teddy Bears"; he applied the term, though, not to the cuddly toys themselves but to bear-shaped automobile accessories. Just a month later, however, in December 1906, the same manufacturer gave us what seems to be the first authentic, properly applied use of the name by which the toy bears were ever afterwards to be known. In another *Playthings* advertisement he offered: "Imported Teddy Bears – best quality with voice $4.50 to $72 a dozen – and also DOMESTIC TEDDY BEARS with voice, Horsman's extra quality $9 to $36 a dozen." In 1907 the New York firm of importers L. H. Mace & Company issued a wholesale

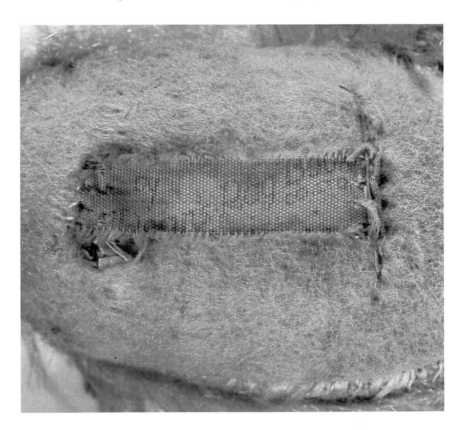

The label stitched into the foot of a Dean's Rag Book bear.

An umbrella stand, 31in (79cm) high, which
caught the author's eye on an antique stall
quite unassociated with bears. (**£80–150;
$132–247**) *Author's collection*

catalogue which offered "plush 'teddy' bears" as distinct from "plush bears" and "Steiff's bears", all on the same page as "puss in boots", "plush elephants", and the "Humpty Dumpty circus".

What seems to have happened is that the end of 1906 and the beginning of 1907 saw in the United States a sudden craze for teddy bears, like that experienced by later generations for hula hoops or Frisbees. Enthusiasm for the toy and acceptance of the name came together. There had been toy bears before – mechanical bears with realistic fur-covered bodies in Victorian England, wooden play bears in 19th-century Switzerland, and carved bears in Russia even earlier – but nothing quite like the teddy bear.

A dark brown "Peter" bear by Gebrüder Süssenguth, which, although supposedly made in 1925, is included in Süssenguth's 1894 catalogue (see opposite). These bears have a metal-edged disc affixed to their chests bearing the words "Peter Ges Gesch no. 895257". (*Ges. Gesch.* is the abbreviated form of *Gesetzlich Geschützt*, indicating that a pattern had been registered or patented, and it is often found on German-made dolls and toys.) The pointed snout has an open mouth, painted in red and white to depict the teeth and palate, and the moving tongue is attached to the painted wooden eyes, which are weighted to move from side to side as the bear is moved. This is a rare bear. (**£200–500; $330–825**) *Sotheby's*

2003/34   2001/34   2004/34   2010/42   2004/34   2001/34   2003/34

ABOVE

This page from Gebrüder Süssenguth's 1894 catalogue shows the company's range of "Peter" bears. Described as a "novelty", the bear is said to have a "most nature-like finish, with movables [sic] eyes and tongue". Süssenguth were manufacturers and exporters of dolls and toys, founded in 1894 at Neustadt-bei-Coburg. The catalogue was in French and Spanish as well as German and English.

LEFT

A most unusual bear by Dean's Rag Book Co. Ltd. On the back of the paper label, which is tied by ribbon to the bear's neck, is a picture of two dogs tearing apart a rag book on which are printed the words "Dean's registered trade mark". Inside the label are the words: "I came from Dean's Rag Book Co. Ltd, 61 High Path, Merton, London SW19. Liberty 2244." Opposite is the legend: "I am a standing honey bear. No. B/981/9." The original price was 27s 6d (£1.37½p), and the bear probably dates from about 1920. (**£60+; $100+**)

Author's collection

RIGHT
Teddy-bear collectors may find themselves collecting all bear-related objects they come across. This wooden standing bear is 12½in (32cm) high, and although it can hardly be called a "teddy bear", it has pride of place in the author's collection. *Author's collection*

OPPOSITE AND OVERLEAF
Teddy-bear chinaware is becoming increasingly hard to find, especially objects decorated with sporting bears – bears playing football, golf, or hockey. Such pieces are sought not only by teddy-bear collectors but by sports enthusiasts also. Even harder to find are examples of teddy bears driving cars or flying airplanes. The ridged, fine china, although unmarked, probably dates from about 1912. The smooth china was made in the 1920s. (**£15–65; $25–100**)
Author's collection

It took a little time for the craze to cross the Atlantic to Britain. Although the London store Gamage's was advertising a variety of soft toys, including bears, in its 1906 Christmas catalogue, it was not using the word "teddy" nor singling out bears for special emphasis. The earliest known reference to teddy bears in Britain is an advertisement of Christmas 1909 for another London store, Morrell's of Oxford Street, featuring "Old Mistress Teddy that lived in a shoe". The red shoe, complete with one large mother bear and twelve small baby bears, sold for one guinea (£1.05).

Many of these early British bears were made by Steiff and imported from Germany, but British toy manufacturers soon jumped on the band wagon. One of the earliest in the field was J. K. Farnell and Company, based in a factory in west London. The firm had for many years been producing stuffed toy animals made from natural skins, but they made

A fine Steiff bear dating from about 1907 together with a photograph of its owner. The bear is 24in (61cm) high. *Sotheby's*

their teddy bears from plush manufactured in Yorkshire. There is something of a mystery about this development. The idea may have come from the Yorkshire textile manufacturer. Perhaps, looking for new outlets for his product, he realized the potential of using plush for soft toys. It seems that the teddy bears – and other animals made by Farnell – were designed specifically to make the best use of plush as a covering. They were high-quality teddy bears on the Steiff pattern and it is even possible that the firm may have had some sort of arrangement – perhaps a licensing agreement – with the German company. (Farnell went on producing their superior soft toys until their factory was damaged by fire in 1934. One of its directors then started up a rival company, Merrythought.)

The fad for teddy bears grew in intensity on both sides of the Atlantic in the years leading to World War I. Teddies appeared in books, in postcards, on Christmas cards, as scrapbook cut-outs. They decorated everything from china to automobiles. They presented themselves in a variety of novel and outlandish forms – they growled, they cried, they nodded their heads, they ran on wheels. There were teddy bears whose eyes lit up electrically. There seemed to be no limit to the manufacturers' inventiveness or to the public's receptiveness. It was a sort of teddy mania and it was brought back to a saner level only by the outbreak of war.

This mechanical novelty was made by the Nuremberg toy-making company Johann Distler. As the bear tricycles forward, the clown spins around on its wheel. The toy is 8¾ × 3½ × 5in (22 × 9 × 13cm).

3.
COLLECTING TEDDY BEARS

Teddy bears have been popular as toys for a long time. Their child owners have lavished affection on them but have not, on the whole, treated them with much respect. They have bitten off their ears, battered their noses, smeared their faces with jam and honey, taken them swimming, shared their baths with them, and, generally, made them suffer. Bears carried by their owners into adult life have not endured this sort of treatment, but neither have they been much cosseted. So the comparatively recent hobby of collecting teddy bears has meant a change of attitude towards the bear; for the first time it has fallen into the hands of someone who wants to preserve it – the collector.

It is in the United States that the largest collections of teddy bears are to be found. The biggest "hug" (the collective noun for teddy bears) in the world is undoubtedly that belonging to Matt Murphy of Texas, who in 1984 was said to have 1,317 bears drawn from 135 different countries. A banker by profession, Matt Murphy has a special room in his house for this enormous assembly, which includes bears made from gold, silver, ivory, leather, walrus tusk, soap, and chocolate. Victor Davis, a San Franciscan real-estate millionaire, is a similarly dedicated collector – he has a hug of some eight hundred bears. Virginia Walker has a large, and ever-growing, collection – over six hundred at the last count – in her house, appropriately named "Teddy Towers", in Florida. In Los Angeles, Mary Ann Rhoads has a hug of over three hundred teddy bears. James Walt, of Flushing in Michigan, who has been collecting since he was fourteen years old, has over two hundred and fifty teddy bears and is known to his fellow collectors as the Teddy Baron.

In Great Britain the largest collection of bears is surely that of a retired army officer, Lieutenant Colonel Robert Henderson of Edinburgh, who has something between four hundred and fifty and five hundred. Colonel Henderson's hug is a uniquely varied one – besides over one hundred of the traditional soft-toy teddies in different sizes, ages, and makes, he has bears in the shape of money boxes, teapots, cruets, candles, paper-weights, chessmen, bottles, cake ornaments, matchboxes, tobacco jars, brooches, umbrella stands, puppets, and ashtrays. They are made from wax, soap, cardboard, wood, china, sugar, gold, silver, brass, and many other materials.

Pride of Colonel Henderson's collection is a 1903 teddy bear which started life as the property of his elder brother. The smallest true teddy bear in the collection is under 1¼in (3cm) tall; the smallest model bear is ⅓in (8.5mm) high. This may be the smallest bear in the world.

The standing bear – 9in (23cm) high – was made by an unknown German manufacturer about 1907. The small – 7in (18cm) – Yes/No bear, dating from about 1920, is also of unknown manufacture. The skittle bear in the centre of the group is rare.
Private collection

Colonel Henderson's bear collection just grew. It is not so much a collection as an accumulation. It contains teddy bears from his own childhood, from his daughter's and from his granddaughter's. Some are souvenirs of his travels abroad, some are presents from friends.

The beginner who sets out to make a teddy-bear collection today must make more deliberate choices. What is he going to collect?

One obvious answer is "old teddy bears". But what do we mean by "old"? One definition of an antique is that it is something a hundred years or more old, but that is a definition of not much help to the bear collector. There is no such thing as a hundred-year-old teddy bear. So to the bear

RIGHT
This 29in (74cm) high white Steiff bear was sold in May 1987 for a world record price of £6,050 ($9,982). It was made about 1904 and has a button in its ear. *Sotheby's*

OPPOSITE
A selection of bear jewellery. Some of the gold and silver items are Victorian, but there are also modern celluloid and plastic pieces. The name brooches can be used on the bears themselves. Stick pins and badges such as these are not so rare that they cannot be picked up quite easily on market stalls. (**£2–40; $3–65**) *Author's collection*

RIGHT
With glass eyes and a button in its ear, this
Steiff bear, standing 24in (61cm) high, was
made about 1920. (**£500–800;**
$800–1,320) *Author's collection*

OPPOSITE
This parade of Steiff bears shows some of
the many colours that were available. These
bears are white, cinnamon, honey, and
beige, and they date from the early 1900s,
about 1920, and the 1940s. (**£300–2,000;**
$500–3,300) *Author's collection*

hunter any teddy bear made before 1940 is held to be an antique. However, bears manufactured after that date, especially those that are no longer made or have changed in style, are still collectible and may still be valuable. And as more and more people are drawn to collect teddy bears, these more modern bears are becoming increasingly sought after.

Many collectors choose to specialize. Some stick to miniature teddy bears, settling on an arbitrary size limit of, say, 6in (15cm). Others go to the opposite extreme and look only for giant teddy bears – human-sized, perhaps, or even life-sized. Others collect only bears with a mohair covering or mechanical bears. Many limit their collection to the bears produced by one company – Steiff, Ideal, Chad Valley, and Schuco are favourites. Some have the ambition to form enormous collections; others

Two rare white Steiff bears wearing leather muzzles and dating from about 1913 were sold in May 1987 for record prices. The left-hand bear, which is 18in (46cm) high, realized £6,050 ($9,982), and the right-hand bear, which is 20in (51cm) high, realized £8,800 ($14,520), a world record. Both bears were in excellent condition and both had the buttons in their ears. *Sotheby's*

prefer to have a small but select hug containing only bears in superb, if not mint, condition.

Obviously, money may be an inhibiting factor for the tyro collector. Early, rare teddy bears will be expensive, as well as difficult to track down. So, if you decide to concentrate on them and have only limited funds your collection will necessarily be restricted. You may well, therefore, decide not to worry too much about age but to go for, say, miniature bears, because these will be more readily obtainable and cheaper. In either case, though, you will almost certainly find yourself caught up in the search for your ultimate bear – the earliest, or the rarest, or the smallest yet.

Vast numbers of teddies have been produced in a vast variety of types, so that the collector has a very wide choice and can still find bargains. His task is probably easier than that of the traditional doll collector. Another advantage the teddy-bear specialist has over many other collectors in the field of toys is that his chosen objects are not particularly fragile – they need little packing and no especial care to transport. This is one reason why their appeal grows steadily among toy collectors, who grow tired of the effort involved in protecting delicate bisque doll's heads or the scratchable paintwork of tinplate toys.

You will need to learn how to recognize a genuine old bear. It is not easy. A young, severely battered bear may at first glance look like a bear of respectable antiquity. But here are some pointers that may help.

Look first at the bear's fur. Most early teddies were made of mohair. There are, though, exceptions to this rule. Some very old bears were made from blanket, which was also a favourite covering for early bears on wheels. Take account of the condition of the covering, which can be an indicator of age – although the balder does not necessarily mean the older. On the other hand be very suspicious if someone offers you an old bear in mint condition. Such bears are few and far between and are very valuable. Yours is much more likely to be, simply, a new bear.

Next look at the arms. Very early bears had extremely long arms. In a genuinely old teddy the paws should reach to midway down the legs and the lower half of the arm should curve away from the body.

The legs, too, will give you some clues. Early bears had very large feet set at right angles to the legs. Very early bears had shaped legs tapering to narrowish ankles, which emphasize the size of the feet still more. After the 1930s the ankle begins to disappear, but the big feet remain almost until World War II.

Most of the larger bears had felt pads on their paws. These pads usually became badly worn in play and they are rarely in good condition on an old bear. If they are badly worn and torn the stuffing may start to fall out and the bear may lose its shape. It may then be harder to date it and to recognize its manufacturer.

Old bears are hump-backed. But a genuinely old bear may have lost its hump because its stuffing has been lost through holes in the fur or because the stuffing has become compacted. You can tell if the hump was

A musical tin bear, 9½ × 4½in (24 × 11cm), made in Germany in the 1920s.

A hug of small bears dating from the 1950s to the present day. The one in blue is a home-crafted bear, as is the one behind it. The bear with the pink ribbon, the red felt bear and the tiny bear in front are all new bears. The tiny yellow bear with the blue ribbon around its neck is an American button bear, beautifully made by Dickie Harrison. Dickie's daughter Donna and her friend Dottie Ayres constitute D. and D. Productions of Baltimore, a company selling craft and antique bears as well as bear accessories. (**£10–50; $16–80**) *Private collection*

OPPOSITE
The right-hand bear is one of the centenary bears made by Steiff in 1980. The edition was limited to 11,000 bears. Each bear is accompanied by a numbered certificate of authenticity. The gray bear, also by Steiff, came from a limited edition issued in 1985. Although there is no certificate, the number on the box in which it was packed corresponds to the number on the tag in its ear. *Private collection*

RIGHT ABOVE
Part of the certificate issued with the Steiff centenary bear illustrated opposite.

RIGHT BELOW
The reverse side of the ear tag of the centenary bear; it carries the same number – 1085 – as the certificate.

6000 EXEMPLARE DIESER EDITION
von langjährigen Mitarbeiterinnen hergestellt wurden, die noch diese alte Kunstfertigkeit besitzen.
In diesem Sinne ist jedes Stück dieser Jubiläumsserie numeriert und von Hans-Otto Steiff handsigniert – als heiter – ernste Erinnerung an eine große Firmengeschichte und als Ausdruck eines bis heute lebendigen Qualitätsprinzips.
Nicht zuletzt aber auch als Referenz an eine „Persönlichkeit", die zum prominentesten Spielzeug der Welt wurde und es bis heute geblieben ist.

Nr. 1085

MARGARETE STEIFF GIENGEN
Erste Filzspielwaren-Fabrik Deutschlands.

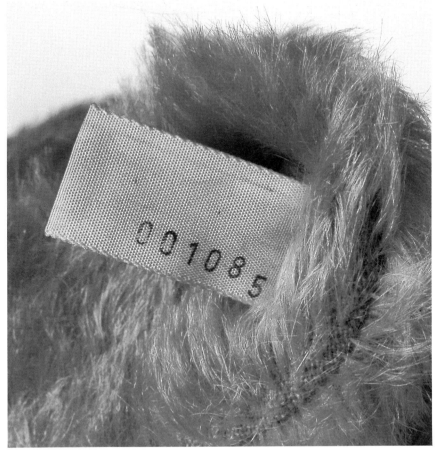

LETS BE CHUMS.

there by gently lifting the fur on the top of the bear's back; you will feel the spare material, like the loose skin of a puppy.

Most pre-1915 teddy bears seem to have had black button eyes. But they may have been pulled out and replaced with glass eyes. So a glass-eyed bear may still be old. You can test by gently feeling around the eyes with your index finger and thumb; if they are so firmly embedded that you cannot move them then they are almost certainly the bear's original eyes.

If you are offered a clothed bear, always insist on removing the clothes so that you can see the condition of the body. Before buying any bear you should check that its head, arms, and legs move freely and go over it carefully looking for holes and tears. Watch out for rips that have been badly repaired – they may give you trouble when you come to clean the bear. But do not be too perturbed if the bear has been patched. As long as the patching has been expertly done the bear will still be resalable.

None of this need bother you, of course, if you decide to collect new teddy bears.

Several manufacturers have made limited editions, replicas of early teddy bears, which are highly desirable possessions and are also good investments. Steiff, for example, in 1980 marked its centenary by producing, in a limited edition, a reproduction of its first teddy bear. Only 11,000 of these bears were issued. Five thousand were given certificates in English; of these, 4,750 were distributed by Reeves International of New York, 50 were held as "specials", and 200 were distributed in English-speaking countries outside America. Six thousand had German certificates, but some of these have now found their way on to the American and British markets. "Papa Bear", as the centenary bear was called, sold then for £35. Today the same bear, in its original box with its

numbered certificate and corresponding ear tag, would fetch well over £300. Steiff also produced, in 1985, a silver-gray bear that cost then about £32. It is already worth about £65 – in other words it has doubled its value in a couple of years.

Merrythought also make covetable limited editions, copies of their 1930s teddy bears.

It is important to remember that these limited editions must be kept in mint condition if you are to look upon them as an investment.

Another mechanical toy by Distler: the bears on the merry-go-round spin around when the clockwork mechanism is wound up. The toy is 10×2×5½in (26×5×14cm).

4.
IDENTIFYING TEDDY BEARS

The teddy-bear collector is not as fortunate as the collector of dolls. Dolls were often indelibly marked by their manufacturers and their variety has been well documented. Unknown teddy bears, whose history has been lost, can be very difficult to identify. Being soft toys, they can have no mark or number permanently impressed upon their bodies. They have often suffered from mistreatment at the hands of their first child owners and may have had ears, eyes, even limbs replaced by conscientious parents.

Experience helps. See as many bears as you can. Go to toy museums and look carefully at labelled, identified teddies. Seek out other collectors and pick their brains. Read books (some are listed in the Bibliography on page 142). Old manufacturers' catalogues and store catalogues with illustrations and descriptions occasionally turn up on second-hand book stalls. These are invaluable to the collector. So too are modern auctioneers' catalogues for sales at which bears were offered.

The notes that follow will help you to identify and date the teddy bears made by some of the more important manufacturers.

BING

The Nuremberg company of Gebrüder Bing began in 1865 as a manufacturer of kitchenware. It started making enamelled tin toys in 1900 and soon afterwards diversified into soft toys. The most sought after of the company's products are the clockwork walking, climbing, and tumbling bears it marketed in the early 1900s. These key-wound bears are today very rare. Many of them were colourfully dressed, sometimes in silk, but to find one still in its original clothing would be a once-in-a-lifetime event. Bing bears carried metal tags marked G.B.N. (Gebrüder Bing Nürnberg) until about 1919 and marked B.W. (Bing Werke) from then on. These tags, like the Steiff buttons (see page 66), have more often than not become separated from their bears. But any mechanical bear with small ears, a flattish nose, and shoe-button eyes should be suspected of being a Bing. The firm went bankrupt in 1932.

CHAD VALLEY

A British company, Chad Valley can trace its beginnings back to 1823 and to a small printing works in Birmingham. In 1897 the firm took over new works beside a stream, the Chad, in a nearby village. It moved into soft toys and dolls during World War I, when it saw the market gap opened up because German-made toys could no longer be imported. In

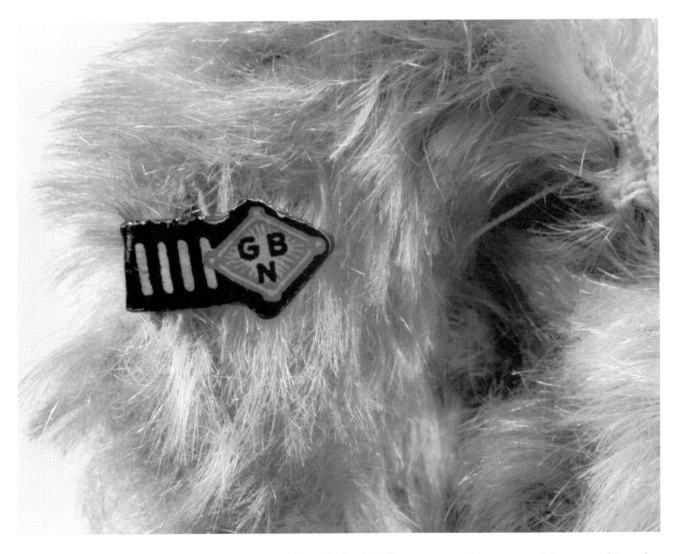

ABOVE
A close up of the tag in the ear of the Bing bear illustrated opposite.

OPPOSITE
This Bing bear, made of white mohair and with black button eyes, stands 16in (41cm) tall. Made about 1910, it is fully jointed and in mint condition. There is a metal tag affixed to one ear with the mark *G.B.N.* (Gebrüder Bing Nürnberg). This is a rare bear.
(**£1,000–2,000; $1,650–3,300**)
Author's collection

1919 it adopted Chad Valley as its trade name and began making also jigsaw puzzles and board games.

The first Chad Valley teddy bears seem to date from around 1920 – the time when the company bought up another small British soft-toy manufacturer, Issa Works. Throughout most of the 1920s Chad Valley produced teddy bears in thirteen sizes and six qualities. Some of them "growled" when tilted – they were fitted with "patent Chad Valley growlers". Some were covered in a particularly brightly coloured mohair – but examples of these are now very hard to find.

Early Chad Valley bears had the by-now-traditional maker's button. This was of metal covered with transparent celluloid and bore the wording "CHAD VALLEY BRITISH HYGIENIC TOYS". The button was not always clipped to its bear's ear – some have been found attached under the arm

or to the front or back of the body. The earliest bears had, in addition to the button, a woven label stitched to the foot. At first the wording on the label – "HYGIENIC TOYS MADE IN ENGLAND BY CHAD VALLEY CO. LTD." – was woven in silk thread. Later it was printed, in red or black. In 1938 Chad Valley received the royal warrant as "Toymakers to Her Majesty the Queen" and changed from a rectangular to a square label to accommodate the necessary new wording. Its current bears carry the label "BY APPOINTMENT TOYMAKERS TO H.M. QUEEN ELIZABETH THE QUEEN MOTHER".

HERMANN

Gebrüder Hermann K.G. began in 1907 and was unusual in that it was set up specifically to make teddy bears. The founder's eldest son left to set up his own company in 1912, operating from a small workshop in Sonneberg, in what is today the German Democratic Republic, then a world centre of toy manufacture. The offshoot company diversified into all manner of dolls in 1927, advertising "dressed double-jointed dolls, Mama walking dolls, unbreakable felt dolls, revue girls, decoration dolls and teddy bears". After World War II the firm was relocated in Hirschaid in the Federal Republic of Germany, and it still produces teddy bears today.

Hermann bears are not easy to differentiate from those made by rival manufacturers. In particular, some of them are hard to distinguish from Steiff bears. Early Hermann bears – which are now very rare – were made of good quality mohair, sometimes in two tones, and were stuffed with excelsior. Both shoe-button and glass eyes are found.

IDEAL

The Ideal Novelty and Toy Company was formed in 1903 to produce in quantity the Morris Michtom teddy bears after the toy wholesalers Butler Brothers had bought up the whole of Michtom's first output and guaranteed his credit with his suppliers of plush. The name was later shortened to The Ideal Toy Company. In 1923 the company was using the slogan, "When we do it, we do it right". Later, its motto became "Excellence in toymaking since the Teddy Bear".

Unhappily, Ideal seems never to have tagged or labelled its bears, so the collector can only judge by appearances – which can be deceptive. Ideal bears are very similar to Steiff bears and can easily be confused with them. Indeed it seems likely that many small early Ideal teddies have fetched over-high prices at auction because they were mistakenly thought to be Steiffs. Ideal bears tend to have wide heads, large low-set ears, and rather pointed feet.

MERRYTHOUGHT

Merrythought began in 1930, when a firm that had been making mohair yarn and cloth, finding its sales hit by the new synthetic fibres that were coming on to the market, looked for new ways of using its mohair products. It came up with the idea of making soft toys. The Merrythought

OPPOSITE
This Hermann bear, made about 1970, is almost identical to a Zotty bear made by Steiff, the only difference, apart from the button in the ear, being the lighter bib patch on the Zotty bear's chest. The Hermann bear is 12in (31cm) high, the Zotty bear 7in (18cm) high. *Private collection*

OVERLEAF
From left to right: a German-made bear dating from about 1920; a novelty bear – when the head is removed, the "tummy" opens to reveal a powder compact; a 1920s bear by the British company Chad Valley; an early German-made bear (as distinct from a "teddy"); an acrobatic bear by Bing, made about 1910 – a spring-loaded mechanism is wound up by rotating the arms; and a honey-coloured bear, bought in Harrods in 1905, with a flat head, shaved nose, long arms, turned-in paws and rather shapely legs with big feet. *Private collection*

company was set up in Ironbridge, the town near the England–Wales border that is named after its prominent landmark, the world's first iron bridge. The first bears produced by the new company carried a celluloid-covered metal ear button depicting a wishbone ("merrythought" is another term for a wishbone) with the words "HYGIENIC MERRYTHOUGHT TOY" printed across it and "REGD. TRADE MARK" and "MADE IN ENGLAND" above and below. The ear button was soon discontinued, on the grounds that it could too easily be confused with the Steiff button. From then on a Merrythought bear was marked only by a label stitched to its foot, machine-embroidered with the words "MERRYTHOUGHT HYGIENIC TOYS, MADE IN ENGLAND". From about 1950 onwards, the labels were printed and the wording changed to "MERRYTHOUGHT, IRONBRIDGE, SHROPS. MADE IN ENGLAND".

SCHUCO

The company that manufactured the famous Schuco bears was founded in Nuremberg in November 1912. The trade name was formed by putting together the first letters of the three words of the company name,

RIGHT
A rare pair of Schuco dark gold mohair bears, which were made about 1950. Both these two-faced bears have black-stitched snouts and metal eyes on one face, and white metal mouths and red plastic tongues and black metal noses on the other face. The heads are turned by means of a brass knob at the base of the body. The bears, which are 3½in (9cm) high, have swivel joints. *Sotheby's*

OPPOSITE
This Schuco bell-hop bear is a Yes/No bear – when its tail is moved from side to side, it shakes its head; when its tail is moved up and down, it nods. Dating from about 1923, this bear is fully jointed and stands 14in (36cm) high. The two small polar bears were made by Steiff. (The Yes/No bear £300–500; $500–800; the polar bears £40–80; $60–130)
Author's collection

Schreyer und Co. At the end of World War I Schreyer opened a new factory in Nuremberg and quickly acquired a world-wide reputation as a maker of ingenious mechanical toys. The firm's teddy bears emerged from this tradition. Schreyer made walking and tumbling bears, key operated. (The keys bore the name "SCHUCO" and so could scarcely be more easily identifiable – to find a bear still with its key, though, would be an event.) It made also teddies whose heads could be made to nod "yes" or shake "no" by using their tails as a sort of joystick.

The Schreyer specialty, though, was miniature bears. In the 1920s the standard height of these tiny bears was 2⅜in (6cm); later versions, introduced in about 1930, were slightly larger – about 3½in (9cm) tall. These miniatures had mohair-covered bodies built up on patented metal frames.

Schreyer und Co. broke up in 1936, when one of its partners, a Jew, fled from Hitler's Germany to England and eventually to the United States. After World War II he and his son formed the Schuco Toy Co. to import into the United States and Canada the products of the re-formed Schreyer company. Schuco toys then became as familiar in North America as they had been in pre-war Europe. But increasing competition from Japan's up-and-coming toy makers ate into the company's profits during the 1960s, and it was declared bankrupt in 1972.

Schuco bears are not normally hard to identify, although dating may be a problem. The nodding-head bears are unique to Schuco.

Steiff used different trade marks at different times. The famous *Knopf im Ohr* ("button in the ear") was introduced in 1905 and is still in use.

OPPOSITE
The Schuco Yes/No bell-hop bear, which is 14in (36cm) high and dates from about 1923, is seen here next to the rare skittle bear and a skating bear. *Private collection*

STEIFF

It is important for the collector to learn how to identify the teddy bears made over the years by this major company. Steiff bears have a style all their own, immediately recognizable by the expert, the clearest features of which are the elongated nose and the slightly humped back. They also

RIGHT
A 1920s Schuco tumbling bear. When it is
wound up, this small bear – it is only 4in
(10cm) high – performs somersaults.
(**£45–80; $75–130**) *Private collection*

OPPOSITE
Made about 1905, this Steiff bear is 9in
(23cm) tall; it is one of the earliest of this size
to have been made. It has no pads on its
arms, only on its feet. (**Mint £200–300;
$330–500**) *Author's collection*

A close up of a blank button in the ear of a
Steiff bear.

carry a very distinct trade mark – a small metal button marked with the
Steiff name that is fixed to the bear's left ear. Over the years, though,
many of these buttons have become detached from their owner-bears and
lost – and many must have been removed and disposed of by parents who
feared that small children might swallow or choke on the buttons.

Steiff bears were marked in this way very early. In 1904 Margarete
Steiff circulated her customers that, from 1 November, "each of my
products, without exception, shall have my trademark '. . . a small nickel
button in the left ear'." Application for registration of this mark was made
by the company on 20 December 1904 and registration officially took
effect on 13 May 1905. The button in the ear is still used by Steiff today.

The front of the label attached to the Steiff centenary bear illustrated on pages 52–3.

The button, when extant, not only establishes its bear as a Steiff, it can also date it. The button's design changed in the course of time, and so did the metal from which it was made, its colour, its size, and its method of attachment. It is possible, if perhaps dangerous, to make a few generalizations. The smaller the button, the older the bear. Buttons with the name "Steiff" in Roman capitals are earlier than those with the name in script. Buttons made from pewter, or from a pewter-type alloy, are earlier than those that are a shining chrome, which are in turn earlier than those made of a brass-like metal. Buttons painted gray date from World War II.

You may be lucky enough to find a Steiff bear with its label still

A fine and large teddy bear dating from about 1948. The large metal Steiff button in its ear is attached to a linen label bearing the number 0339/15. This rare bear has an open, pale orange mouth of felt, a stitched, short snout of blonde plush, and large brown and black glass eyes. The pricked ears are rounded. The bear, which has swivel joints, is stuffed with straw, and the large, rather flat and short feet are of blonde plush with black-stitched claws. It stands 64in (163cm) high, and it was made as a display bear for a German department store. It is probably the largest jointed Steiff bear in the world. (**£3,000+; $4,950+**) *Sotheby's*

attached (the button pinned the label to the ear). The labels, too, changed over the years. White labels date the bear to before 1926; red labels to 1926–34; yellow to 1934 onward; and white-and-yellow or black-and-white to the present day – not earlier than 1980. The less information the label carries, the earlier it is.

The four-figure numbers on a Steiff label bear a great deal of coded information about the animal (not necessarily, of course, a bear) to which they are attached. The first figure defines the animal's posture. 1, for example, denotes a standing animal. 3 means a sitting posture. 5, the number most likely to be found on a teddy bear, signifies "jointed". The second numeral tells the material with which the toy is covered. 1 is felt, 3 is mohair, 5 is plush, 6 is Dralon. The last two figures give the animal's height in centimetres – quite simply, the final figures 34 would mean a toy 34cm (13in) high.

Sometimes the four-figure number is followed, after a comma or an oblique stroke, by a single numeral. This reveals how the animal is equipped. 0 means that it is *not* on wheels. 1 means that it has a voice box and 3 that it has a music box. These single numbers may occur in combination.

These generalizations about buttons and labels are not hard-and-fast rules. You will need to research more carefully to date more precisely. In any case, the probability is that your bear will have lost its label and button. Or it may have acquired the wrong button (Steiff sometimes seems to have found a stock of old buttons and used them out of order). Or someone may have put a Steiff button on a non-Steiff bear. So you will need to be able to recognize also the changing body-styles of Steiff bears. The more humped the back, the longer the nose, the longer the arms, and the bigger the feet, the earlier the bear. But, again, this is a generalization that should be taken with a generous pinch of salt.

Undoubtedly, the best way to learn about Steiff bears is to visit the company's museum at Giengen-am-Brenz in West Germany. Here there are hundreds of original Steiff animals and dolls in mint condition – teddy bears still with their tags, elephants, dogs, cats, giraffes, and camels. Here too are all the catalogues the firm has issued and about 20,000 glass negatives from which the catalogue illustrations were made. This is a researcher's paradise.

Visiting museums that have collections of teddy bears is always a good way of improving your recognition skills. Make a point of visiting the museums in your district and try to check also on any museums in the area when you go away on business or on vacation. Listed on page 77 are some collections that have teddy bears on display in Australia, the United Kingdom, and the United States. Obviously, though, this is a highly selective list – many other museums in many countries will have collections that are well worth seeing. You should watch out particularly for those museums that have the words "doll" or "childhood" in their titles.

This Steiff mechanical tumbling bear, 12in (31cm) high, dating from about 1915, is in mint condition: there is still some of the white label attached to the button in the ear. (**£800–1,300; $1,320–2,145**) *Author's collection*

Another view of the Steiff tumbling bear.

The left-hand bear is a Steiff brown plush bear on wheels. Made about 1920, it has a disc in its ear. The protruding, rounded muzzle is black stitched, the glass eyes are brown and black, and the rounded ears are set far apart. The growling mechanism is activated by a metal pulley on the shoulders. The bear stands on metal stretchers attached to solid wooden wheels, one of which is missing. It is 19¼in (49cm) high. (**£300–400; $495–660**)

On the right is a small beige plush bear on wheels, which was made about 1907. It has a pointed snout, short ears and a tail, and it stands on metal stretchers attached to metal wheels. The eyes are missing. It is 9in (23cm) high. (**£250–300; $412–495**) *Sotheby's*

"A gentle reproof": a postcard printed in England and posted on 2 May 1910.

MUSEUMS

Australia
The Teddy Museum
118 Edward Street
Brisbane
Queensland

United Kingdom
The Bethnal Green Museum
Cambridge Heath Road
London E2

The London Toy and Model Museum
23 Craven Hill
London W2

The Museum of Childhood
38 High Street
Edinburgh

Museum of Childhood
(incorporating Playthings Past)
Sudbury Hall
nr. Derby
Derbyshire

National Toy Museum
The Grange
Rottingdean
nr. Brighton
Sussex

Pollock's Toy Museum
1 Scala Street
London W1

United States of America
Aunt Len's Doll and Toy Museum
6 Hamilton Terrace
New York 10031

The Carrousel Museum
Midland
Michigan

Children's Museum of Indianapolis
3000 N. Meriden Street
Indianapolis 46208

The Margaret Strong Collection
Manhattan Square
Rochester
New York 14607

Memory Lane Doll and Toy Museum
Old Mystic Village
Mystic 06355
Connecticut

Museum of Old Dolls and Toys
Chesterfield Road
West Chesterfield 03466
New Hampshire

Museum of Old Toys and Dolls
1530 6th Street NW
Winter Haven 33880
Florida

Perelman Antique Toy Museum
270 S. 2nd Street
Philadelphia 19106
Pennsylvania

5.
ACQUIRING TEDDY BEARS

How should you set about building up your teddy-bear collection?

New bears can be found easily enough in any toyshop. For the more unusual bears – if you have decided to collect only battery-operated bears whose hearts can be felt beating or only those whose eyes light up – you will have to look a little farther afield than your local toyshop. In Britain, Hamley's in London's Regent Street, the country's largest toyshop, stocks countless varieties of bears, as do the big London department stores, such as Selfridge's or Harrods, that have large toy departments.

For antique, old, or commemorative bears you will have to find other sources.

The first place to look is in your own home and the homes of your friends and relatives. Now that people tend not to stay in one place for very long and to live in smaller houses and flats than their parents did, the chances of finding an unexplored, dust-covered attic full of family treasures has become rather remote. But it is always worth looking – and asking. Perhaps an aunt or a grandmother will confess that she has never found the heart to throw away some child's much-loved teddy.

Next, extend your area of search by going to local fêtes and bazaars, jumble or rummage sales, and garage sales. Again your chances of any great discoveries may not be high, but as more and more people begin to appreciate that teddy bears are collectible, and therefore salable, so more and more are being dug out and offered for sale.

Markets are always worth a visit. The author, who is based in London, has spent many happy hours, and found some bears, in three markets in particular – those in the Portobello Road, Camden Passage, and Camden Lock. The Portobello Road market is held every Saturday, from 6.30 a.m. to about 4.00 p.m. Its stalls wind their way from near Notting Hill Gate underground station towards Ladbroke Grove and sell every conceivable kind of antique and collectible. Camden Passage market opens twice a week, on Wednesdays from about 5.30 a.m. to 2.00 p.m. and on Saturdays from 8.00 a.m. to 4.00 p.m. Wednesday is the day for trade dealings; Saturdays seem to appeal more to amateur collectors, who come to browse as well as to buy. This is an interesting and varied market, a mixture of shops and stalls, in arcades and in the open, where you can find collectibles of all kinds, from heavy furniture to delicate jewellery. Its nearest underground station is the Angel. Not far away is Camden Lock market, which straggles out to Chalk Farm. It is open on Saturdays and Sundays from about 7.30 a.m. to late afternoon. Several bears now in the author's collection were bought at Camden Lock.

Standing 16in (41cm) high, this cinnamon Steiff bear was made about 1905. The shorts and vest are newly made, and the miniature boxing gloves, which must have been a traveller's sample, have the words "Baily's, Glastonbury" printed on them. The author bought them in a flea market. (**£200–300; $330–500**) *Author's collection*

OPPOSITE
A Steiff bear, which is also illustrated on pages 84 and 85. *Author's collection*

OVERLEAF
It can be both great fun and something of challenge to dress your bears and to find outfits that suit them. *Author's collection*

BELOW
Collecting accessories for bears can be almost as enjoyable as collecting the bears themselves. Victorian dog collars, miniature whistles, fob watches, spectacles and even an eye glass can be used to give your bears character. *Author's collection*

Look out, too, for the toy and doll fairs that are held periodically at various venues, usually in big hotels. In London, one of the largest is run by Brenda and Steve Clark of Grannies Goodies; it is attended by almost all the established teddy-bear dealers. Another fair, held at the Cumberland Hotel, is organized by Wendy Enever and is particularly popular with foreign dealers. Another is run by Anthea Knowles; it is an annual two-day show held round about the third week in May. The first day is reserved for the trade, the second is open to the public and is attended by serious collectors from all over the world. Finally, but importantly, there is the Living Dolls toy fair, run by Carol Stanton and held about four times a year at the Hilton Hotel in Kensington.

Then there are the teddy-bear rallies. Although buying and selling is not their primary purpose, some permit market stalls. And even when there is no official selling, well, whenever bear collectors are gathered together there is always the opportunity to do some dealing. These gatherings have now become commonplace and frequent in Britain, the United States, Australia, France, and Germany. One of the earliest was held in England on 21 May 1979 at Longleat, the stately home of the

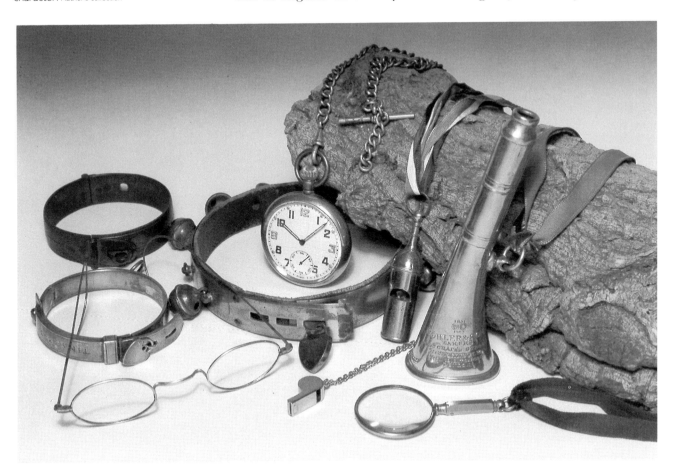

This 1913 Steiff bear is very rare. It is seen here with and without its muzzle. The bear is 10in (26cm) high. *Author's collection*

Marquess of Bath. This "Great Teddy Bear Rally and Honey Fair" attracted over 8,000 visitors. It was even reported in *Time* magazine, under the headline "Arctophilia Runs Amok". (Teddy-bear collectors had for some time been calling themselves "arctophiles", lovers of the bear.) A second such jamboree at Longleat, in 1983, was even more successful. In the same year, in the United States, the 80th anniversary of the appearance of the teddy bear was celebrated by a monster rally held on 25 July at the Philadelphia Zoo and attended by some 25,000 people. (The managing director of the Steiff organization was one of the visitors; he appeared with the firm's 1902 prototype teddy bear chained to his waist for security reasons – it was reputedly insured for $40,000.) Other, less ambitious rallies have been held at the London Zoo and at the London Toy and Model Museum, at Liverpool (in aid of the National

Society for the Prevention of Cruelty to Children), at Timsbury (in aid of the National Children's Homes), and at Stratford-on-Avon.

Another source of teddy bears is the auction room. Sometimes teddy bears are auctioned in mixed sales along with other antiques, but an increasing number of auctions are now being devoted either to toys including dolls and teddy bears or to dolls and teddy bears alone. Normally the bears will be on display for one or two days before the sale and you should always attend this preview to see what is on offer. Go around, catalogue in hand, make notes, and decide, before you find yourself caught up in the heat of bidding, what you are prepared to pay. This is the time to ask questions, if you need more information than the catalogue gives. Remember, when you decide the limit of your bid, that, in Britain, you will be charged a "buyer's premium" of 10 per cent on

This honey-coloured purse dates from the 1940s. It is fully jointed and lined with rexine; the handle is narrow grosgrain ribbon. The maker is not known. (**£100–200; $165–330**)
Author's collection

The left-hand bear was made by Steiff about 1913; it has its original muzzle and is 13in (33cm) high. The right-hand bear, also by Steiff, dates from about 1908 and is 11in (28cm) high. The basket-work pram, which is 28in (71.5cm) long and dates from about 1890, makes a delightful prop for the bears. (**Each bear £500–800; $825–1,320**)

Sotheby's

your successful bid and that, in the United States, you may have to pay a local sales tax of up to about 8 per cent of the price.

Now that teddy bears have moved up-market they are put on the auction block by some of the world's most prestigious auction houses – and they are beginning to fetch appropriately high prices. At one sale held in London by the internationally renowned firm of Christie's in December 1986 some two hundred teddy bears, in 150 lots, bought in a total of £16,600. The highest price reached was £1,650 for a 24in (60cm) high Steiff bear, "with defective growler", dating from about 1909. Several Steiff bears from the 1950s fetched over £100. Earlier in the same year, in June, Sotheby's had sold a 30in (75cm) Steiff bear of 1904 for £4,800. In 1987, at sales outside London, a large plush Steiff bear of 1905

The left-hand bear is an early Steiff curly plush bear, 20in (51cm) high and dating from about 1904. The right-hand bear is a black German-made bear, 14in (36cm) high and dating from about 1908.
(**Each bear £1,000+; $1,650+**)
Author's collection

LEFT
A German-made musical tin toy, which is 13½×7½in (34×19cm).

Also German, this mechanical toy has a clockwork action that causes the bear to strike the rods attached to the balls and so make them spin around. The bears left arm rises and falls.

fetched £990 and a smaller Steiff dated to 1915 made £748, while a hump-backed bear of an unusual gray-green colour, thought to be an early Steiff, went for £1,300.

Buying a teddy bear may, if you are susceptible, be rather like buying a puppy. You may find yourself tempted to give a bear a good home because you are touched by the pathetic way in which its head lolls forward or its arms fall limply to its sides. It may seem to have a "happy" expression which cheers you up or a "sad" air that cries out for comfort. No amount of advice can help you in these circumstances. If the bear appeals to you in that way, you will probably buy it. Try to remember, though, that you are buying not for the nursery but for a collection. Before you commit yourself and part with your money do examine the bear coolly and thoroughly. Try to identify it accordingly to the hints given in Chapter 4. Check its condition, making sure that its joints – at neck, shoulders, and hips – move freely, that its fur and pads are reasonably whole, and that it has not lost too much of its stuffing.

And try to appraise realistically what you will have to spend on it, in time and money, to put any defects right.

6.
THE CARE AND REPAIR OF TEDDY BEARS

When you bring home a newly acquired old bear for your collection you must first of all treat it almost as though it were a real, live animal – you must quarantine it. The reason is that you cannot be sure where it has been or know what it has picked up. It may be carrying parasites that could attach themselves to your resident teddy bears – some bears found in attics and lofts are infested with moths, silverfish, or even fleas. You can hardly be too careful. Whole teddy-bear collections have been ruined by moths and other insects, which find teddy-bear fur an ideal breeding ground.

It is a wise precaution, therefore, to seal the bear in a plastic bag and

This rather battered and worn Steiff bear, which dates from 1908, is the author's lucky mascot. It should stand on a metal wheeled base, but it is far too fragile for any restoration work to be attempted. (**£50–200; $80–300**) *Author's collection*

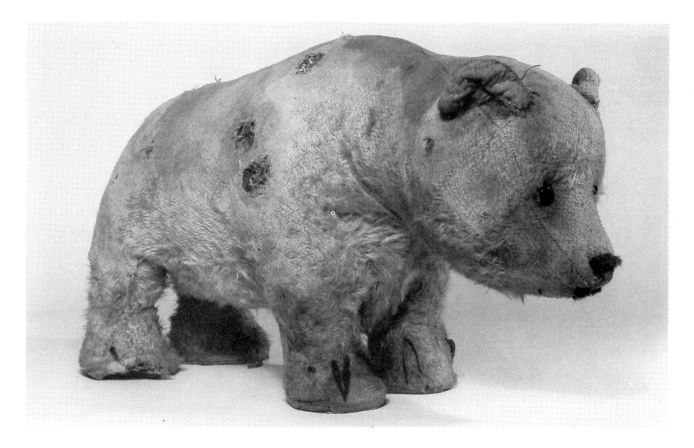

This Steiff bear, dating from about 1910, has the typical elongated snout and humped back. It has been restored – notice the nose and ankle, for example, and the top of the leg – but this has not detracted from its value. It is 29in (74cm) high. (**£1,000–1,500; $1,650–2,500**) *Author's collection*

This is the Steiff bear illustrated opposite before restoration.

put it in the freezer for 48 hours or more. This should kill off any foreign bodies. If you seal the bag tightly the bear will not get wet, but no lasting damage will be done if the seal is imperfect and the bear does get a little damp. Dry it carefully with a hair dryer (on gentle heat) or leave it in an airing cupboard overnight and it will completely recover. If it emerges from the freezer not damp, but merely very cold, let it stand at room temperature, like a bottle of wine, for a few hours before you begin on any necessary cleaning or repair work.

Now you can safely examine the newcomer to see what treatment it needs. The first task is normally to clean it, but it is a good idea to check first for split or open seams or for obvious damage to the fur. Serious rips and tears in the covering are best repaired before cleaning, to avoid the risk of losing any more stuffing, but if the bear is very dirty you may

This 1907 Steiff bear on a metal wheeled base is in good condition. It stands 9in (23cm) high. (**£250–350; $412–575**)
Author's collection

prefer to tack the tears together with a few rough stitches and leave more permanent repairs until it has been cleaned.

It is, of course, much easier to clean a more modern bear than a pre-1930s vintage bear. The fabric used to cover newer bears is usually spongable, if not washable. Older bears were made of less easily cleaned (and less durable) materials, such as mohair. (There is a glossary of materials used in bear-making on page 140.) However, there is no need to leave even a very old and fragile bear in a matted and dirty condition. Provided you use the right tools and exercise care and patience you can safely restore it to something like its pristine glory.

A light Steiff bear dating from about 1912. It is 24in (61cm) high and has a button in its ear. At auction in May 1987 it fetched £750 and no doubt received the attention it rather obviously requires. *Sotheby's*

Begin by brushing the bear all over with a bristle brush, taking particular care around the eyes and muzzle. It is important that the brush be not too hard; it should have firm but pliant bristles. Nor should it have any sharp edges which might tear the fur. Never, incidentally, use a brush that you have used on your own hair, because oils from human hair can cause a static reaction with synthetic fabrics, such as plush, that may form the bear's covering. The same reaction occurs if you use the same brush for mohair-covered and plush-covered bears – mohair is a natural fibre like human hair. It is best to keep two separate brushes if you regularly have to clean both types of bear.

No one has yet marketed a special teddy-bear cleaning liquid. Use a liquid soap made for delicate fabrics, slightly diluted, and work it gently into the fur with a brush. A softish toothbrush or nailbrush is ideal, unless you are dealing with an outsize bear. Apply the liquid sparingly, trying not to get the fur too wet, "fussing" it in with a circular motion. Leave it for a short time and then buff the bear all over with a soft hand towel, which will absorb the grime loosened by the cleaner. Repeat the washing process, this time using tepid water to which a little fabric conditioner has been added (follow the manufacturer's instructions for the proportions). Again, lightly towel the bear down.

The bear must now be thoroughly dried. One way is to use a hair dryer (on a low setting), directing the warm air over the fur while gently brushing it down. Or you may leave the bear out in the sun for a few hours – no more or sunlight may begin to fade the fabric of the covering. Or put it in a warm airing cupboard for a day or two.

Once dry the bear should be brushed, with both upward and downward strokes, fairly briskly, but with a soft-bristled brush.

Any necessary repairs should now be carried out. Rents in the fabric should be neatly sewn or darned, but before you close any tears carefully tease out the stuffing inside to restore the shape. Similarly, sew up any open or torn seams with strong cotton thread. Bald patches on the fur are best left alone – any attempt at patching is likely to make the situation worse. Many of the larger bears had felt pads on their paws and these are very often badly worn or scuffed. Sometimes they can be patched, but it may be better to replace the whole pad. You can usually buy small pieces of felt that are a close enough colour match in the haberdashery departments of the larger stores. Do not cut out the old pad, simply stitch the new one over it.

It is not uncommon for bears to have lost one or both of their eyes, or to have unsuitable ones substituted for the originals. Replacing eyes is a job well within the do-it-yourself capacity of most amateurs. Glass eyes can be purchased readily enough and it is relatively easy to "spike" them into the head. Since the bear is not going to be a child's plaything it is not quite so essential to ensure that there are no sharp points that could do harm. The black button eyes sported by very old bears are more of a problem. You will have to search flea markets and second-hand clothes shops to find the old boot and shoe buttons – the sort that button hooks were intended for – that make ideal replacement eyes for small and medium-sized bears. Once found, though, it takes no great skill to sew them into position.

Some late 19th-century dolls were given teeth, made of porcelain, glass, or even bamboo. Over the decades these teeth have often been damaged or lost, so that the doll collector sometimes has to practise renovative dentistry. The teddy-bear collector is luckier – teeth are very rarely a problem to him.

Some research has, however, been done on the teddy bear's dental problems. On 1 April 1980 the *British Dental Journal* published a paper,

This Steiff bear, which dates from about 1905, is in lovely condition. The paws must have been restored many years ago, for the leather used is old. The feet have been more recently repaired. It is 21 in (54cm) high. (**£400–800; $660–1,320**)
Author's collection

A large Steiff bear – 30in (76cm) high – dating from about 1902. It is in fairly good condition apart from having some stuffing missing from the tip of its snout, the top of a leg and from both ankles. One pad has also been replaced. (**£800–1,500; $1,320–2,475**) *Sotheby's*

"Dental Disease in *Brunus edwardii*", by Barry Scheer, B.D.S., L.D.S., of the London Hospital Medical College Dental School. The paper "discusses the problem of dental diseases in *Brunus edwardii* and correlates its prevalence with dietary patterns of the species and its association with humans." Professor Scheer cites evidence from Milne (1928) that teddy bears have "a craving for excess carbohydrate in the form of honey" and suffer "psychological disturbances which are associated with territorial disputes with Tiggers and Heffalumps and even small children". He set

out to test the hypothesis "that the predilection for foods containing a high sucrose content in *Brunus edwardii* would give rise to the dental diseases with which humans are already familiar". He examined a random sample of teddy bears in the London area and found that in "72.8 per cent of all bears at least one tooth was affected by caries".

There is no need for this to disturb us. The toothed teddy bear is very rare, perhaps fortunately. One example – a "laughing Roosevelt Teddy Bear" of 1907 – opened its mouth when its stomach was pressed, revealing a set of vicious-looking white glass teeth. It is singularly horrid.

Your sanitized, cleaned, mended, patched, re-eyed bear is now ready to take its place in your collection. If any more demanding repairs, or any serious restoration works, are needed it is probably best to entrust your bear to an expert. A very few names of some teddy-bear repairers are listed below.

A collection of travellers' samples including a collapsible opera hat – 7in (18cm) high – a beautiful silver-gray top hat – 6in (15cm) high – several trilbies, a straw boater and a cap, which is 4in (10cm) long and 3in (7.5cm) wide. The smallest of the briefcases is 4×2×¾in (10×5×2cm). Such items are difficult to find, but they are well worth the effort. (**From £10; $16**) *Author's collection*

SOME TEDDY-BEAR REPAIRERS

United Kingdom
Bristol Dolls' Hospital
Alpha Road
Southville
Bristol
Avon

The Dolls' Hospital
16 Dawes Road
London SW6

Minutiques
82B Trafalgar Street
Brighton
East Sussex

United States
The Dolls' Hospital
787 Lexington Avenue
New York
NY 10021

Enchanted Valley Doll's Hospital and
Bear Refuge
1700 McHenry Village Way
Modesto
California 94303

The Grizzlies
223 W. Lloyd Street
Pensacola
Florida 32501

You must make sure that, having cleaned your bears of any pests or parasites, they stay that way. You must take steps to see that they are not reinfected. The most obvious preventative is the old-fashioned moth ball, but this has a penetrating smell which some people find unpleasant. Moth-proofing sprays are obtainable from some drug and hardware stores. Herb-filled muslin bags can also be tied to the bears if they are on open display, or placed beside them in the cupboards or trunks in which they are stored.

A fine orange-coloured Steiff bear with a button in its ear. This is a very rare and covetable colour, and the coat is in excellent condition despite showing some wear. Some of the stuffing in the snout and arms has moved. The bear is 27in (69cm) high. (**£1,500–2,000; $2,475–3,300**) *Sotheby's*

7.
ASSOCIATED BEAR COLLECTIBLES

Many collectors have concentrated not on teddy bears themselves but on related items – what might be called beariana. There is an immense variety to choose from.

What became known as the "teddy-bear fad" in the United States began as early as 1906. It became fashionable then to have a teddy bear decorating the side lights of automobiles. In the same year one of the first of the bear spin-offs was marketed by J. & E. Stevens Company of Connecticut; it was an iron money box – Teddy, the bear bank.

Clothes for bears began to be produced very quickly, to cash in the new toy's popularity. Still in 1906, two American firms, Kahn & Mossbacher and W. Shoyer & Co., were in competition with a full range of clothes for the well-dressed teddy bear. Within a few years it was possible to buy bear underwear, nightwear, sailor suits and clown outfits. Knitting and sewing patterns enabled conscientious mothers and bear-loving daughters to make their own "teddy clothes". It was soon possible to buy teddy-bear wardrobes to store these outfits – as well as chairs for teddy to sit in and beds for it to sleep in. The problem for the collector, though, is that it is often impossible to determine whether these clothes and this

"Bear and forbear": unfortunately there is no indication on the card itself of when and where it was posted.

OPPOSITE
This is the cinnamon Steiff bear illustrated on page 78. The Macfarlane Lang biscuit tin dates from about 1910; it is $7\frac{1}{2} \times 3\frac{1}{2} \times 4\frac{1}{2}$in ($19 \times 9 \times 11$cm). *Private collection*

A chocolate mould of standing bears; it
measures 14 × 8in (36 × 20cm) and is
made of tin. *Author's collection*

equipment were meant for teddy bears or for dolls. Often, of course, they did double duty.

Teddy bears were soon surrounded by other accessories. The Lloyd Manufacturing Company of Michigan offered circus carts and cages for teddy bears. Pedal cars for teddy bears to drive were offered by Hamburger & Company.

Writing in the American antiques magazine *Spinning Wheel* (April 1971), Emma Stiles records that the teddy-bear craze went so out of control that manufacturers were making all kinds of toys carrying the teddy-bear name or exploiting the teddy-bear image. There were teddy-bear teasets. There were puzzles, card games, and box games. There was teddy-bear stationery. There were teddy-bear muzzles, leashes, balls,

The three wooden bears with bases are chess pieces; the two standing on the left are 3½in (9cm) high, and the "piggy-back" bear on the right is 3in (7.5cm) high. The seated bear with the two glass bowls is part of a cruet set; the bear, also wood, is 2in (5cm) high. *Author's collection*

Bath night for two Steiff bears. The bath is enamel and probably dates from the Edwardian era. The inside of the bath is decorated with bears going about their everyday activities, and there is a hole at one end to hang it up. The bath, which is unmarked, is 27½in (70cm) long and 8in (20cm) high. (**£70–150; $115–250**)
Private collection

hammocks, balloons, rocking horses, pins, rubber stamps, water pistols, bricks, even teddy-bear brief cases made of plush. Teddy bears seemed everywhere.

By 1909, in Britain and the United States, the teddy bear was no longer merely a child's toy. It was a fashion accessory. At seaside resorts ladies promenaded carrying large buff, brown, or pale yellow teddy bears. Even in 1906, *Playthings* had reported seeing teddy bears accompanying young women in Central Park, New York. At a fashionable Paris hotel, bears sat at table sharing a meal with their owners. Some were even lavishly bedecked with expensive jewellery.

Greetings and Christmas cards featuring teddy bears became popular in the years leading up to World War I and offer an interesting – and as yet not well documented – area for a collector to investigate. Most of the Christmas cards of the period are predictable and orthodox – they show teddy bears being given to happy children by benevolent Father Christmases, awaiting their new owners under Christmas trees, or simply

RIGHT
Three table bears. The brass bear on the left is an ink-well; its head is the lid and lifts up to reveal the ink. It is 3in (7.5cm) tall. In the centre is a corkscrew made of composition; there is also a cover in similar material that fits over the screw; it is 5½in (14cm) high. On the right is a chrome table lighter; the fuel-impregnated wick is stored in the bear's body and threaded through the "cigar" in its mouth ready to be lit. It is 4½in (11cm) high. (**Each £10+; $16.50+**) *Private collection*

OPPOSITE
These birthday-cum-postcards of children and their teddy bears date from the 1930s and were among the earliest to depict the age of the child for whom they were intended. The right-hand and lower cards were printed with the greetings "Thinking of you and wishing you joy" and "Wishing you every joy today" respectively, and they were postage paid – 1d.

OVERLEAF
This delightful lamp, which was made to resemble a teddy-bear shop with little bears in the window and this author's name on the front, is coveted by many. Made by a friend as a gift, it is beyond price. *Author's collection*

as loved toys in nursery scenes. Easter cards tested the artists' imaginations more – a stress which produced some occasional delights, such as an enormous bear emerging from an egg and being confronted by two startled chicks asking (as well they might), "Who are you?".

There was also a flood of bear postcards. The arrival of the teddy bear coincided with perhaps the peak of the European enthusiasm for sending postcards. The custom had developed in the 19th century, as the extension of railway networks made travelling easier and cheaper than ever before, so that more and more people wanted to keep in touch with distant homes. Communication by postcard was then encouraged by the ever-growing efficiency of postal services and made less expensive by the invention of new printing techniques that allowed photographs to be reproduced in great numbers very cheaply. One great boost to postcard senders in Britain was given by the Post Office, which in 1894 reduced the cost of sending a postcard to one halfpenny. Four years later, in America, the postal charge for postcards was reduced from 2 cents to 1 cent.

Among American publishers were Edward Stern of Philadelphia and

Three teddy thimbles that would be as keenly sought after by collectors of sewing paraphernalia as by collectors of teddy bears. The thimble on the left with the bear seated on a tablecloth is made of metal. The bear's arms are jointed. The thimble in the centre is also metal, but painted to resemble pottery, with a bear apparently seated on a log and eating a picnic. On the right is a beautifully made silver thimble, with bears running around the outside and one seated on top. All three are 1 ½in (4cm) high. Thimbles such as this may be obtained through thimble clubs and silver craft shops. (£8–20; $13–30) *Private collection*

I am having a good
BLOW
at GUERNSEY

HUNSTANTON.

Ask me anything in reason
but don't ask me to
leave this Plaice!

What! Come Home?
Not likely, when I'm at
Llandudno!

Teddy bears rapidly became favourite subjects for
postcard artists. The card from Guernsey was posted
in July 1912 and the example from Hunstanton,
England, in July 1914.

The best of friends I hope you'll be
And never quarrel or disagree.

"Baby's Plate"

SILVERHAIR — ! DECLARE YOU HAVE BROKEN BRUINS CHAIR!
WHEN THEY REACH THEIR HOME (OR LAIR):-WHEN THEY SEE THE HAVOC THERE:-
T'WILL BE MORE THAN THEY CAN BEAR.

THE THREE BEARS

BABY'S PLATE

The front cover of the sheet music of Bonheur's *The Teddy Bear's Frolic.*

PRECEDING PAGES, LEFT
This delightful plate is unmarked, but it is known to have been manufactured in the 1920s. It is a very rare item, of the kind that appeals to both doll and teddy collectors. (**£45–70; $75–115**) *Author's collection*

PRECEDING PAGES, RIGHT
This plate was manufactured by Shelley about 1903. It has great charm – especially the tiny bear on wheels being pulled along by the baby bear. (**£45–70; $75–115**)
Author's collection

Both these silver bears were made about 1904. The baby's rattle on the right is in mint condition: it has a bone teething ring and a mother-of-pearl handle, and two bells are attached to the bear's arms. It is 7in (18cm) long. The jointed bear with a muzzle on the left may have been part of a child's plaything, but, as a child might easily have bitten off an arm or a leg, it seems more likely that this very rare item was part of a chatelaine. It is 2½in (6cm) high. *Author's collection*

BELOW AND BELOW LEFT
Perhaps the most famous of all teddy-bear tunes was *The Teddy Bears' Picnic*, for which the American composer J. E. Bratton wrote the music in 1907; the lyrics were written in England by Jimmy Kennedy.

FUN O... ...MATES.

A BANDY CHAIR.

Among the spate of teddy-bear cards published immediately before World War I were those produced by C. W. Faulkner, which was founded in 1900 and which used

a spray of vine leaves as its trade mark. Of
the cards illustrated here, postmarks can be
deciphered on three – one showing 1909
and two, 1910.

Mabel Lucie Attwell achieved great success with the postcards she designed for Valentine & Sons at the start of World War I.

B. E. Mooreland. In Britain, the firm of Raphael Tuck, founded by a Prussian immigrant named Tuch, became the leading producer of cards by the beginning of the 20th century. Other well-known British companies were Bamforths, of Yorkshire, founded in 1870; Valentine & Sons, of Dundee, who began to print postcards in 1897; and C. W. Faulkner, founded in 1900.

In the course of time some artists began to specialize in drawing for the postcard trade. In America, Richard Felton Outcault specialized in "Buster Brown and his dog, Tige"; in Britain, Mabel Lucie Attwell concentrated on chubby children and Donald McGill cornered the market in saucy seaside postcards. All these artists drew teddy bears.

The commonest of teddy-bear postcards simply show children at play with their bears – bathing them, dressing them, generally caring for them. Most are highly sentimental and anthropomorphic – "My Teddy nearly always cries because the soap goes in his eyes." Some are instructional. There is a Donald McGill, very much out of the ordinary run of this artist's normal bawdy humour, in which a mother bear and two baby bears are sitting at table, having tea. Mother is saying "How

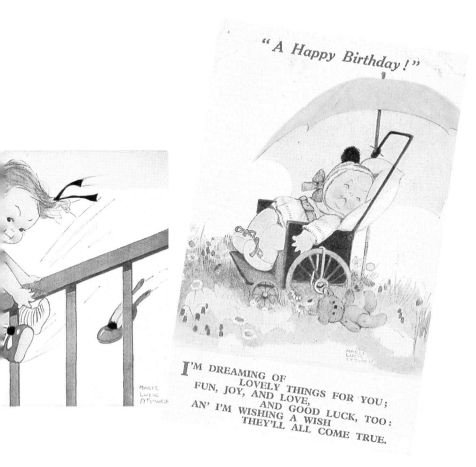

"*A Happy Birthday!*"

I'M DREAMING OF
LOVELY THINGS FOR YOU;
FUN, JOY, AND LOVE,
AND GOOD LUCK, TOO:
AN' I'M WISHING A WISH
THEY'LL ALL COME TRUE.

often am I to tell you to put your paws in your lap and not to growl till you're growled to".

Away from children and into the world of Edwardian passion, postcard teddy bears are often used to send romantic messages. One example has a teddy bear rushing into another's arms and is captioned:

> "I love you dear" says Teddy
> "Far better than my life
> So make me happy sweetheart
> And say you'll be my wife."

Another — more McGill in spirit, though it is not a McGill — has a stereotype spinster sitting up in bed beneath a sampler reading "I'm longing for someone to love me" and hugging a teddy bear. The title is "Her Last Resource".

The occasional topical, political allusion turns up. A McGill has a teddy-bear policeman arresting a teddy-bear suffragette and saying "Come along, Christabear!"

Then there are the standard jokes translated to the world of teddy

Cake decorations are often made in the form of bears and are an ideal subject for collectors with only limited space. The two bisque characters date from the 1920s and the Christmas figure from the 1940s. (**From £5; $8**) *Private collection*

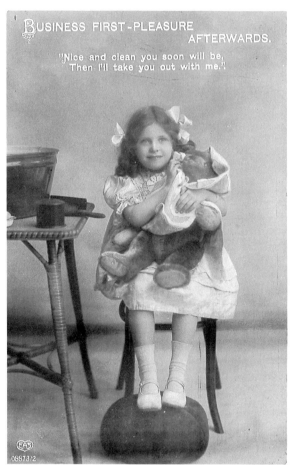

BUSINESS FIRST - PLEASURE AFTERWARDS.

"Nice and clean you soon will be,
Then I'll take you out with me."

THE PRIDE OF THE FAMILY.

"To be a real smart Teddy-Bear,
I ought to comb and brush your hair."

Look at Mrs. Teddy Bear,
Don't she make you laugh?
To see her getting ready
Teddy for his bath.

LEFT
This wall-hanging bear, which is 8in (20cm) high, has a string running down its back. When the string is pulled, the bear's arms and legs shoot out to the sides, making the bear appear to jump. (**£5–20; $8–30**)
Author's collection

OPPOSITE
The two top cards were printed in Germany by the London-based company E. A. Schwerdtfeger & Co., whose monogram – E.A.S. – is visible on the left-hand card. The lower card was printed in Britain in the aptly named "Popular" series.

bears. There is even a mother-in-law joke – a blood-curdling illustration of a teddy bear falling from a primitive airplane is captioned:

> We gave a slight cough
> When Teddy's Mother-in-law slipped off
> the "Curtiss" Aeroplane.

Perhaps commonest of all, though, are cards showing teddy bears engaged in ordinary human sporting activities – bathing, playing golf, skating ("the ice bears beautifully"), or sailing toy boats. There is at least one practical, or useful, card. It is simply a drawing of a teddy bear with,

ABOVE
The author's "shop clock". Made by Smiths in the 1940s, the clock still keeps good time. When it is wound up, the bear's head nods giving the impression that the bear is striding along. *Author's collection*

OPPOSITE
The Steiff bear dates from about 1903 and is 13in (33cm) tall. The tin has the words "Berlingots Carpentras" printed on it, and it is decorated with bears all the way round. (**£300–350; $500–570**) *Author's collection*

over its rump, a small patch of sandpaper. The invitation accompanying this is:

> If for a smoke you are inclined
> Just Strike a Match on the Bear behind.

Early in the teddy bear's history, enterprising companies seized upon it as an ideal sales symbol – its comforting image conveying associations of safety and security and homeliness. In 1909 Peak Frean biscuit delivery vans on the streets of London had 36in (90cm) high bears

Bear Brand advertising material is extremely collectible. The left-hand bear, raising a top hat, dates from about 1950. It is made of cardboard and stands 6in (15cm) high. The smaller bear – 4in (10cm) high – is also made of cardboard, but its legs are attached by a washer and can be made to rotate.
(**Each £1–2; $2–3**) *Private collection*

perched on their roofs. These promotional bears were made by Ralph Dunn and Co. of the Barbican, London. The teddy-bear motif was used by the company until the 1970s. Bear Brand stockings of Chicago still have a Chad Valley bear, made at the British factory in about 1905, as their trade mark. The original was recently auctioned in London by Sotheby's. "Cosy" was the bear mascot for a Coal Utilization campaign in Britain in the 1960s. He sat in many coal merchant's windows to draw attention to the advantages of solid-fuel central heating. The Russians chose a teddy bear as their symbol for the Moscow Olympic Games in 1980.

WHOSE SHOE CAN THIS BE?

Here's pretty pussy with some very nice toys As presents for good little girls and boys.

Best Wishes

READY TEDDY GO!

Family Railcard

ABOVE
Even British Rail found the teddy bear a potent advertising symbol.

LEFT ABOVE AND LEFT
"Whose shoe can this be?" appeared in a series of cards produced by "Boots Cash Chemists"; this particular card was posted in 1909, while the greetings card was sent in 1912.

8.
FICTIONAL AND FAMOUS TEDDY BEARS

Bears have, of course, featured in the literature and romance of the Western world for centuries and have a special place in the folklore of many nations – especially, and not very surprisingly, of Russia. Perhaps the best known of these folk tales is that of the three bears, an old story that for a long time was believed to have been first recorded by the British poet Robert Southey somewhere between 1834 and 1837. At this time Southey was nearing the last years of his life (he died in 1843) – years, says the *Oxford Companion to English Literature* rather unkindly, "marked by an increasing mental decline". Recent research however has shown that there is an earlier, manuscript, version of the fable, pre-dating Southey's by at least three years and written by an otherwise unknown author, Eleanor Mure. The book – *The Celebrated Nursery Tale of the Three Bears, put into verse and embellished with drawings for a birthday present to Henry Broke, September 26, 1831* – is now part of the Osborne Collection of early children's books in the Toronto Public Library.

The three bears were not, of course, three teddy bears. The teddy bear had to be invented in reality before it could be imagined in literature. But having been invented it was not long before it was seized upon by the writers of children's fiction.

The American writer L. Frank Baum peopled his magical world of Oz with bears who are clearly not just any old bears but contemporary teddy bears. A brown bear in *The Lost Princess of Oz* (1917) was "chubby as well as fuzzy; his body was even puffy, while his legs and arms seemed jointed at the knees and elbows and fastened to his body by pins or rivets. His ears were round in shape and stuck out in a comical way, while his round black eyes were bright and sparkling as beads." Accused of being stuffed with sawdust, he retorts with some indignation, "I am stuffed with a very good quality of curled hair and my skin is the best plush that was ever made."

The most famous teddy bear in fiction was taken from the shelves of the toy department in London's most prestigious store, Harrods, in 1920. A young mother, Dorothy Milne, bought it as a present for the first birthday of her son, Christopher Robin. She was the wife of Alan Alexander Milne, a journalist, novelist, and essayist who had been assistant editor of Britain's pre-eminent humorous magazine, *Punch*, until the outbreak of World War I and had just embarked upon a new career as

OPPOSITE
London Zoo's much-loved polar bear inspired a book-ful of songs. This likeness appeared on the back cover of "Brumas Tunes".

a playwright. His *Mr Pim Passes By* had already been a West End success. The newly acquired toy bear soon became part of the family. It was an English bear, made by J. K. Farnell, and it was at first given an English name, Edward. It was re-christened with a name obtained by combining Christopher's name for his favourite bear at the London zoo, "Winnie", with that for a swan he used to feed on a lake near the family's home in Sussex, "Pooh". The idea of writing Winnie-the-Pooh into stories for children is said to have come to A. A. Milne one day when an actor, Nigel Playfair, was visiting the Milnes. Christopher came down from the nursery, saw the visitor, and exclaimed, "What a funny man! What a funny red face!" Admonished, he denied that he had spoken; the rudeness, he claimed, had been perpetrated by Pooh. So Pooh came to literary life – together with some of Christopher's other soft toys, a piglet, a donkey, and a tiger.

Later in life Dorothy Milne remembered acting out incidents in the stories with Christopher's Pooh and his other nursery animals. She described how the boy would say to his father, "Come and see me in my bath and then you can read the latest story to Pooh." This delightful picture is, however, rooted more in wifely loyalty than in truth. Christopher himself, many years later, revealed that "Strangely enough, although my father wrote so much about me, he did not like children. . . . In fact he had as little to do with children as possible. I was his only child and I lived upstairs with my Nanny. I saw very little of him. It was my mother who used to come and play in the nursery with me, and tell me about the things I thought and did. It was she who provided most of the material for my father's books. . . ."

Christopher's early years were made unbearable by his identification with the Christopher Robin of his father's stories and verses and his association with Pooh. Taunts of "Where's your teddy bear?" followed him throughout his unhappy schooldays. And yet, ". . . as far as I can remember I knew nothing of the stories until they were published. Then my Nanny used to read them to me. . . ."

Pooh first appeared between the covers of a book in *When We Were Very Young*, published in 1924. Two years later, in 1926, he had a book to himself – the eponymous *Winnie-the-Pooh*. This is without much doubt the best-selling teddy-bear book of all time. It has been translated into 22 languages (including Esperanto and the Initial Teaching Alphabet). In America alone over ten million hardback copies have been sold in the sixty-odd years since its publication. In Britain the paperback still sells over one hundred thousand copies a year. It is also a best seller in Russia, where over four hundred thousand copies of *Winni-Pukh* have been sold in the last ten years. Even the Latin translation, *Winnie Ille Pu*, by Alexander Lennard, became a cult best seller in the United States, spending twenty weeks on the *New York Times* best-seller list in 1961.

In 1928 Milne related more of Pooh's adventures in *The House at Pooh Corner*, which was another instant success. One dissenting voice was that of the American journalist and wit Dorothy Parker who, reviewing

Winnie Ille Pu, translated by Alexander Lennard, was first published in Britain in 1960 and became an unlikely bestseller.

this latest addition to the Pooh canon, said that she got only as far as page 5; then, she claimed, "Tonstant Weader Fwowed Up."

All the Pooh books were illustrated by Ernest Shepard, whose vision of Pooh has become the image imprinted upon all our minds. Milne, who knew Shepard's work from a time when they had both worked together on *Punch*, thought his style was unsuitable and had to be persuaded that he was the right man for the job. In the event it was as much Shepard's drawings as Milne's words that turned the Pooh books into nursery classics. The model for the Pooh illustrations was not Christopher's Pooh but Growler, a teddy bear belonging to Shepard's small son.

On 5 February 1968 one of Shepard's original Pooh drawings fetched £1,200 when it was auctioned by Sotheby's in London. When he was 90 Shepard gave his pencil sketches for the Pooh drawings to London's Victoria and Albert Museum. The original Pooh bear for long resided with Milne's American publisher, E. P. Dutton, but now sits in the New York Public Library's Central Children's Room.

A strong contender with Winnie-the-Pooh for the winner's trophy in the nursery-classic stakes has emerged in Paddington Bear. Certainly Paddington must now be the highest-earning bear in the world, for he has an income of over five million pounds a year from the rights to use his

Winnie-the-Pooh has so far appeared in four animated films made by the Walt Disney Company. Here he is seen in two scenes from *Winnie-the-Pooh and the Honey Tree.* The reception accorded to the animated version of this most famous of bears was, in England at any rate, mixed, probably because perceptions of Pooh's character and appearance are based on long familiarity with Ernest Shephard's inimitable illustrations. ©*The Walt Disney Company*

name on over two hundred products ranging through badges, stickers, T-shirts, wallpaper, furnishing fabrics, and chocolates. He has been translated to television in Britain and the United States and has recently been reincarnated as an educational computer game.

Paddington has enjoyed, after a slow start, a meteoric rise to fame. His adventures are today published in more than twenty languages. Yet he is a comparative newcomer. He appeared mysteriously on Paddington rail station in London in 1956, having arrived from Peru, and was found sitting in his duffel coat, Wellington boots, and felt hat with a label pinned to him, "Please look after this bear. Thank you." Michael Bond got the idea for Paddington one Christmas Eve when he was looking for last-minute presents in Selfridge's store in London. He saw a single teddy bear left on a shelf. "I thought the bear looked so lonely that I bought him as a Christmas present for my wife," says Michael Bond. Ten days later he wrote a story about the bear. Five publishers turned it down before it was published two years later.

Bully Bear, although not as widely known nor as popular as Paddington, will be familiar to all knowledgeable teddy-bear collectors. He existed as a toy before becoming a character in books. The brainchild of Peter Bull, in association with Alison Wilson, Bully Bears are produced by the House of Nisbet. They are deliberately designed to look "old-fashioned", with humps and pronounced snouts. Bully Bear now has two siblings, Young Bully (who wears the regalia of the Worshipful Company of Peanut Butter Eaters) and Bully Minor. The first Bully Bear book, written by Peter Bull, appeared in 1981 and had the bear carrying the bride's train at the wedding of Britain's Prince of Wales to Lady Diana Spencer. In succeeding books Bully Bear went to a teddy-bear rally at Longleat, became a punk, went to Hollywood and starred in a commercial for peanut butter, and became a doctor and went on a fact-finding expedition to Australia (to establish whether koala bears qualify as teddy bears). All have been illustrated by Enid Irving.

Preceding all these was Rupert, the foremost cartoon-strip teddy bear. His adventures have been appearing in the British daily newspaper the *Daily Express* for nearly seventy years and have also been published in at least eighteen languages other than English. Rupert Bear and his friends from the village of Nutwood were first created by the illustrator Mary Tourtel. She was a faintly larger-than-life character who was an aviator and adventurer as well as an artist. She was commissioned to produce a competitor to Teddy Tail, a popular cartoon character appearing in a rival newspaper, the *Daily Mail*. Animals had been a feature of several of her already-published children's books, so she was an unsurprising choice. She came up with an anthropomorphic "Little Lost Bear". The captions in verse that accompanied the drawings were written by her husband, who happened to be a sub-editor on the *Express*:

Two Jolly Bears lived in a wood   One day his Mother sent him off
Their little son lived there too.   The marketing to do.

Rupert, who first appeared in the *Express* on 8 November 1920, was soon joined by his friends Bill Badger, Algy, Edward Trunk, Podgy Pig, and the Wise Old Goat – who at one time was the most popular character in the strip. In a short space of time Rupert became a children's national favourite, with his own fan club, the Rupert League.

In 1935 Mary Tourtel's sight began to fail and she had to give up her work on the Rupert strips. Her replacement was Alfred Bestall, a cartoonist and book illustrator. It is said that he was less than pleased, having accepted the commission, to realize that the job meant not only drawing the strip but thinking up and writing the stories. Editorial policy forbade the appearance in the tales of any frightening or really vicious villains, any evil magic, or any behaviour by Rupert that might set a bad example to children. Working within these restrictions, Bestall sent Rupert away from his Nutwood home into mythical foreign countries and introduced a new science-fiction element into the stories. Nonetheless, every story began and ended with Rupert back home, in the reassuring presence of Mrs Bear. Bentall produced the strip for thirty years, until his retirement in 1965. During the whole of this time Rupert only twice failed to appear in the *Express* – once when he was crowded out by one of Winston Churchill's wartime speeches and once when Pope John XXIII died in 1963.

Although Bentall continued to contribute to the Rupert annuals until 1973 (he died at the age of 93 in January 1986), after his retirement the strip was taken over by various artists. It is now written and drawn by Jim Henderson. Through the years, and through a number of illustrators, a remarkable uniformity has been maintained.

Rupert's name has been used to sponsor all manner of products, including children's clothes, furniture and furnishings, tableware, other toys, jewellery, and confectionery. Rupert has his own television series and has been played on stage. W. O. G. Lofts and Derek J. Adley, who have compiled a Rupert bibliography, *The Rupert Index*, estimate that nearly one hundred million Rupert books have been sold.

Rupert has recently been in the news again, through the cartoon film *Rupert and the Frog Song*, made by ex-Beatle Paul McCartney, which became a hit video.

Very much in the tradition of Rupert is another toy-animal hero in the strip-cartoon mould – SuperTed. Dreamed up in 1974 by Mike Read, and based closely on Superman, SuperTed uses his magical power to protect small children.

SuperTed's image is very different from that of an older media bear, Sooty. Sooty started life as an ordinary glove puppet that entertainer Harry Corbett bought in 1949 from a toyshop on the pier of the British seaside resort of Blackpool. He called it simply "Teddy" and used it in his act at children's parties. When, a few years later, he appeared with the bear on British children's television, he was instantly popular and soon had his own show. Sooty, too, became the star of a strip cartoon and replicas, made by Chad Valley, were soon available in toyshops. Sooty, who got his name because the original glove puppet had a smudge of black on his snout, is now a fully fledged international television personality.

The first real teddy-bear television star, though, was Andy Pandy's teddy. Andy Pandy is a child-clown, but a clever one; it is Teddy who invariably gets into trouble. Andy Pandy first appeared on television in the programme *Watch with Mother* in 1950, but it was not until the following year that Teddy made his bow. He was made by Chad Valley and had loose-jointed limbs so that he could be operated as a puppet. The Andy Pandy stories were told by Maria Bird, simply and with simple props. Films featuring Andy Pandy, Teddy, and their friend Looby Loo, a rag doll, have been for some reason especially popular in Australia and New Zealand. Stories about the trio now appear in a number of children's comics throughout the world.

Teddy bears as bit-part players in adult fiction occur with surprising frequency. As Peter Bull has said, ". . . it would be impossible to list *all* the books in which Teddy Bears are mentioned and frightfully boring if I did." He cites, nonetheless, Jean Genet's *Our Lady of the Flowers* (1940), Aldous Huxley's "The Gioconda Smile" (1922), and Ian Fleming's *Casino Royale* (1953).

Best known of all teddy bears in literature is surely Aloysius, the companion of Lord Sebastian Flyte in Evelyn Waugh's *Brideshead Revisited* (1945). The narrator, Charles Ryder, describes his first glimpse, in the Oxford of the 1920s, of Sebastian:

> My first sight of him was in the door of Germer's and on that occasion I was struck less by his looks than by the fact that he was carrying a large teddy-bear.
>
> "That," said the barber as I took his chair, "was Lord Sebastian Flyte. A *most* amusing young gentleman."
>
> "Apparently," I said coldly.
>
> "The Marquis of Marchmain's second boy. . . . What do you suppose Lord Sebastian wanted? A hair-brush for his teddy-bear; it was to have very stiff bristles, *not*, Lord Sebastian said, to brush him with, but to threaten him with a spanking when he was sulky. He bought a very nice one with an ivory back and he's having 'Aloysius' engraved on it – that's the bear's name."

Charles and Sebastian become friends. They go for a drive in Sebastian's car:

> Sebastian's teddy-bear sat at the wheel. We put him between us – "Take care he's not sick" and drove off.

And Charles receives a letter from Sebastian:

> "I've a good mind not to take Aloysius to Venice. I don't want him to meet a lot of horrid Italian bears and pick up bad habits."

In the television film of *Brideshead Revisited*, the part of Aloysius was played by a teddy bear belonging to Peter Bull. An American bear, its name was Delicatessen, because it had sat for 55 years on the shelf of a

dry goods and grocery store in Sacco, Maine, before it was given to Peter Bull in 1969. As Aloysius, Delicatessen won a special award from the magazine *Time Out* "for the best performance in the most trying circumstances". In Hollywood the bear received the ultimate accolade of stardom – its pads were impressed in the cement outside Grauman's Chinese Theatre. On 21 February 1982 the bear's name was formally changed to Aloysius by deed poll ("sealed and delivered by the above named Aloysius after the document had been read over to him and he appeared perfectly to understand and approve").

The teddy bear does not seem to have impressed the poets – verse references to it are few and far between. Some verses of excruciating mawkishness have been written for children, but the only poet of stature even to mention the teddy bear was Sir John Betjeman, in the lines quoted (on page 7) at the beginning of this book. Betjeman's teddy bear was not, of course, fictional – he was a real bear belonging to a real boy – so these lines are a piece of real reporting, which absolves them from sentimentality.

One of the best known and best loved of literary bears is Michael Bond's Paddington, who arrived from Peru in 1956.

The late Sir John Betjeman's lifelong companion was Archibald Ormsby-Gore, and Betjeman's own sketch of Archie is shown here on a letter to him from doll and teddy-bear authority Mary Hillier.

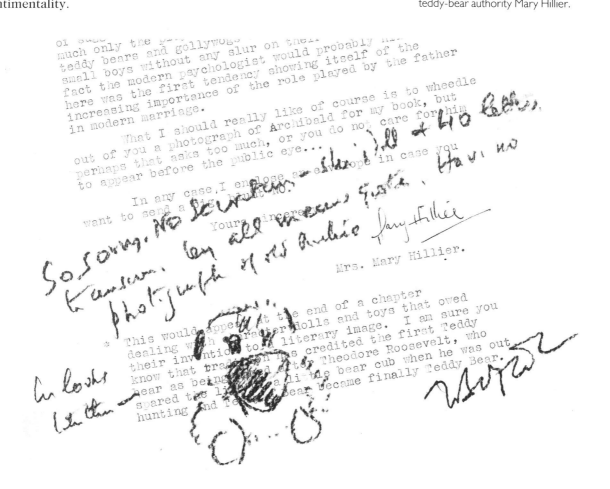

A GLOSSARY OF SOME MATERIALS USED IN BEAR MAKING

acrylics   synthetic textile fibres made into washable cloth for modern bear coverings

burlap   a coarse, heavy fabric woven from jute or hemp and used as a covering for some early stuffed toys. In Britain it is more commonly called hessian

excelsior   a trade name, registered in 1868, for fine, curled wood shavings used as stuffing in many early soft toys

felt   a pressed cloth of wool and sometimes fur matted together; often used for bears' pads

gutta-percha   a tough plastic substance, like rubber, made from the latex of several trees; often used for bears' snouts

kapok   the silky fibres that cover the seeds of the kapok tree; used as stuffing around the voice boxes of some early bears

mohair   a fabric made from the long, silky hair of the Angora goat; luxurious and dirt-resistant it is a high-quality covering for soft toys

plush   a fabric rather like velvet, but with a longer and less dense pile. It can be made to imitate fur, and was therefore much used as a teddy-bear covering

rexine   a material rather like oilcloth often used for the pads of early British-made bears

velveteen   a cotton material made with a short pile in imitation of velvet, sometimes used as bears' fur

OPPOSITE
The Schuco clockwork skating bear, which is also illustrated on page 67, was made about 1920. Standing 10in (26cm) high, it glides along as if skating when wound up. This example is in good condition.
(**£200–500; $330–825**) *Private collection*

BIBLIOGRAPHY

Bialosky, Peggy and Alan, *The Teddy Bear Catalogue*, Workman
  Publishing, New York
Bull, Peter, *Bear with me. The Teddy Bear: a symposium*, Hutchinson,
  London
——, *A Hug of Teddy Bears*, The Herbert Press, London
Hillier, Mary, *Teddy Bears : a Celebration*, Ebury Press, London
Mullins, Linda, *Teddy Bears Past & Present: a Collector's Identification
  Guide*, Hobby House Press, Cumberland, Maryland
Waring, Philippa and Peter, *Teddy Bears*, Treasure Press, London
——, *In Praise of the Teddy Bear*, Souvenir Press, London
Wilson, Jean, and Conway, Shirley, *Steiff – Teddy Bears, Dolls and Toys*,
  Wallace-Homestead Company, Iowa

Periodicals

The Doll and Toy Collector, International Collectors Publications,
  Swansea
The Teddy Bear and Friends, Hobby House Press, Cumberland, Maryland

INDEX

Page numbers in *italics* refer to captions to illustrations.

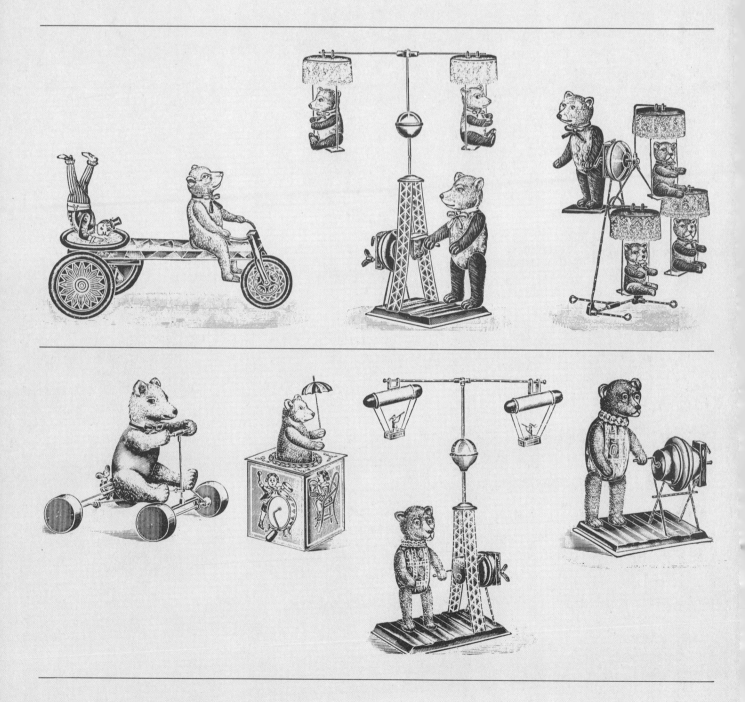